# Trainsp

## North West

C000181741

## Contents

# About the book

So here we are with book 3. This time we are looking at the north west corner of England. With some beautiful open landscapes, coast lines and urban outskirts to provide a mixed set of locations. The book marks the first collaboration with a local photographer whose help in the creation of this edition has been immeasurable. My sincerest thanks go to Mark for all the miles and hard work he's put in.

**Marcus Dawson**
**Hertfordshire**
**June 2010**

After offering to help with my 'local' edition I now have a keen understanding of the amount of work that goes into producing these books. There are many locations we could have included but space did not permit this. I would like to dedicate this particular edition to the well known local photographer Don Burgess who unfortunately died in 2009 and who was my guide to finding many of the locations featured here.

**Mark Bearton**
**Lancashire**
**June 2010**

## HOW DOES THE BOOK WORK?

### Chapter Information

Gives information about the traffic flows for the section of line covered. However, these are subject to change without notice and should be used as a guide only (especially freight workings).

### Location Notes

Gives general information about the area - the surroundings, the amount of road traffic, the type of people likely to be encountered, whether wellies will be needed.

### Public Transport

Since not everyone has a car, these notes give information on using public transport.
All public transport information is correct at the time of writing. Walking times are given as a guide only. Bus services and frequencies shown apply to Monday to Friday daytimes only. Weekend and evening services may be different or non existent.

Bus routes and times can change at short notice so please always check before travelling. Recommended public transport planning tools are:

http://www.nationalrail.co.uk/       http://www.transportdirect.info/
http://www.taxiregister.com/       or you can telephone Traveline on 0871 200 2233.
The destination bus stop, where noted, is indicated by a ⑧

### Amenities

Gives information on toilets, places to eat and other local facilities that can be reached easily from the location.

### Accommodation

Gives information on places to stay nearby, if any.

### Photographic Notes

Gives information on the times of day* that provide the best light conditions, the height of the bridge parapet, whether a step ladder would be useful, whether there is enough room to stand and for a video tripod and what sources of noise would interfere with audio recordings.
Each picture contains details of the time, month and lens so the photographer can plan ahead. In order to make this book, each location has been revisited and checked within the last 2 months and the pictures are representative of the current shot available. If there are any changes they have been noted in the text. All photos were taken by Mark Bearton unless otherwise stated.

*Any times quoted represent the summer months when the sun rises early and sets in the late evening. These should be taken as a guide as the sun will rise or set outside these times during certain months of year.*

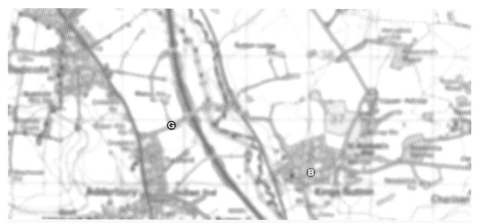

**Postcode: X00 0XX**  **Lat N00:00:00**  **Long W00:00:00**

## Sat Nav information and Road directions

The postcode provides a reference for your Satellite Navigation system. This will take you to the place indicated by the Ⓖ on the map which will be close to the location. If it is not on the location, use the map for the last few yards. These post codes did not include house numbers so if a house number is requested, please ignore it. They were checked using a 2010 Garmin Nuvi system. Other systems should provide similar results.

The location is always at the centre of the map and the Latitude and Longitude provide an absolute reference to this point.

The map squares represent a 1 kilometre scale, which is approximately 2/3rds of a mile.

## Acknowledgements

This book would not have been possible with out help and original input from:

Eliot Andersen, John Balaam, Ian Ball, Scott Borthwick, Jack Boskett, Denis Bradley, Tony Callaghan, Ken Carr, Ron Carr, David Dawson, Peter Foster, Neil Gibson, Carl Grocott, Neil Harvey, Fred Kerr, Murray Lewis, David Maxey, Andrew Naylor, Chris Nevard, Richard Norris, Adam Parkinson, Steve Philpott, Sarah Power, Anthony Roberts, Richard Stiles, Richard Tearle and Andrew Wills

And I would also like to echo Mark's sentiments in dedicating this book to the memory of Don Burgess.

## Important Note

Advice about the general environment of each location is given on each page. This information is a guide only. Always be careful. Avoid leaving your property on display and be aware of your surroundings at all times. There are, sadly, people who will not think twice about trying to steal your equipment.

# WCML - Warrington to Carnforth

## General Notes

The line is a mixture of two and four track sections, passing through several urban areas and also long sections of countryside. In the four track sections the slow lines are situated on either side at Winwick and then on the western side north of Euxton. The entire route is electrified with 25kv Overhead wires.

## Passenger Traffic

Virgin Trains operate two trains per hour in each direction along the route, one being a Pendolino from London and the other a Voyager from Birmingham.

Various other operators use sections of the line. Arriva Trains Wales 175s can be seen near Warrington, Trans Pennine Express 185s north of Euxton and various second generation Northern units throughout the whole length, though they are only infrequent between Preston and Lancaster.

The Caledonian sleeper also uses the route, this normally operates during the hours of darkness.

## Freight Traffic

Intermodal Anglo-Scottish trains are the staple traffic along the length of the route operated by DB Schenker with 92s, Freightliner with 86s and Direct Rail Services with 66s.

In addition there is coal traffic from DB Schenker and Freightliner as well as infrastructure trains from both operators.

Royal Mail class 325s operate several times a day, these workings can also be operated by loco hauling the units.

DRS operates a daily flask train. Colas Rail's log train from Carlisle to Chirk can be seen, though these occasionally run via Settle and when doing so only join the WCML south of Preston.

## Occasional Traffic

The route is popular with special excursions heading for Carlisle or Scotland.

The West Coast Railway Company has its base at Carnforth so is a source of regular Empty Coaching Stock trains to other parts of the country to form rail tours.

The Network Rail 'New Measurement Train' HST has a weekly diagram along the route.

1) 180108 at Farington with a northbound evening service.
*April, 18:30, 80mm*

2) 60004 with a northbound Enterprise working at Winwick.
*January, 13:15, 115mm*

3) WCRC's 47760 heads south at Brock with charter ECS.
*April, 10:00, 130mm*

# WCML - Warrington to Carnforth

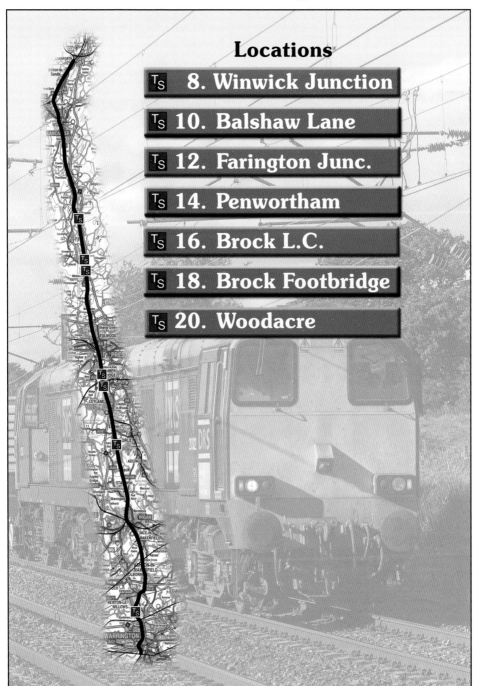

## Locations

- T̲s̲ **8. Winwick Junction**
- T̲s̲ **10. Balshaw Lane**
- T̲s̲ **12. Farington Junc.**
- T̲s̲ **14. Penwortham**
- T̲s̲ **16. Brock L.C.**
- T̲s̲ **18. Brock Footbridge**
- T̲s̲ **20. Woodacre**

# Winwick Junction

## Location Notes

A popular train watching and photographic location a few miles south of Warrington. The bridge carries a lane over the railway and offers views in both directions. Whilst the lane is fairly quiet you do get the odd lorry passing. It is also popular as somewhere for people to park to eat their lunch.

1) Apart from a palisade fence in the foreground, the shot has changed little since 1995 when 91001 headed south on test.
*Photo by Neil Harvey, June, 19:30, 50mm*

## Public Transport

Arriva, service 329, operates half hourly between Warrington Bus Station and St. Helens to Hollins Lane in Winwick. If travelling from St. Helens alight at first stop after you cross the Main Line. From Warrington alight at the stop immediately after the hospital on Hollins Lane.

## Amenities

There are none at the location itself. The Fiddle I'th Bag Inn is located on the road to Burtonwood just west of the railway and serves good pub meals.
The A49 to Warrington has a range of fast food restaurants and supermarkets along its length.
Snack Bars can be found in the industrial estate to the south-east.

## Accommodation

There is a Premier Inn located on the A49 by the junction with the M62.

## Photographic Notes

The light is best here for southbound trains from early morning, on the eastern side of the bridge, to late morning continuing on until late afternoon for the western side, after which it favours northbound workings, but from the western side. To the south of the bridge there is a palisade fence, but from the bridge this will not mask anything in shot. It would, however, make track level shots impossible without a step ladder. There are bushes along the length of the lane but the fence is not high so a step ladder would not be required. The verges are also wide enough to set up video tripods so only the sound of the occasional car or lorry on the road behind would affect audio sound tracks.

# Winwick Junction

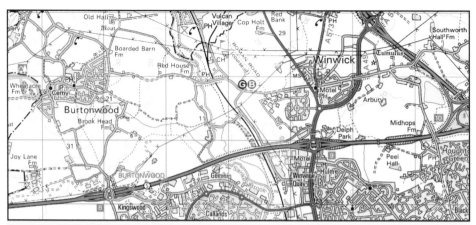

**Postcode: WA2 8RY**          **Lat N53:25:36**          **Long W02:36:56**

## Road Directions

From the M6, Junction 22: Take the A49 towards Warrington and Newton. At the next roundabout, after a mile, turn right onto the A49 towards Newton. After about half a mile, opposite the large church, turn left into Hollins Lane towards Burtonwood. You pass a small hospital on the left and after this take the first left into Watery Lane. The bridge is located on the first lane on the right (Old Alder Lane) at the brow of the hill. There is space to park your car on the verges on either side of the bridge.

2) 60074 heads south with a rake of former-National Power hoppers on the Liverpool-Fiddler's Ferry circuit.
*October, 12:15, 80mm*

# Euxton, Balshaw Lane Junction

## Location Notes

The location comprises two footbridges across the line in a rural area immediately south of the point where the slow and fast lines merge. The line here used to be four tracks with the two remaining lines on the east. There is little shelter and the footpaths can become very muddy so stout shoes are advisable.

1) From the northern bridge. 66843 heads south with the loaded Carlisle to Chirk logs
April, 16:45, 50mm

## Public Transport

The nearest railway station is Euxton Balshaw Lane from where it would be about a 20-25 minute walk. Buses from Chorley also stop near the railway station, but there are no stops closer to the location.

## Amenities

There are no amenities at the location. There is a good pub, the Euxton Mills, located at the roundabout on the main road.

## Photographic Notes

The line here is roughly north to south so the sun will be head on around midday. The northern, first, bridge is better for northbound trains due to the southern orientation of the steps. The downside of this is you will be shooting into the light. The second bridge has north facing steps so the southbound shot here will be better. In the morning the angle is very tight as the lines are opposite the steps. However, in the afternoon the angle opens up from the

2) 390035 speeds northwards with a Glasgow working
January, 13:00, 80mm

western steps. The overhanging tree growth does mean you need to be high up the steps.

Both bridges are in a very quiet area with few people passing so would be good for videoing; the lines gradient is climbing for southbound trains, so trains will be accelerating after negotiating the junction. Whilst the overhead wires can be a problem the head span catenary is not too intrusive.

# Euxton, Balshaw Lane Junction

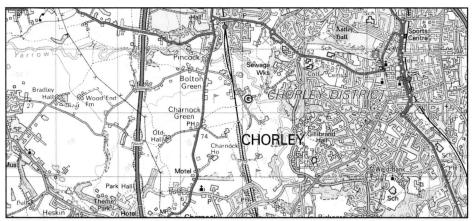

**Postcode: PR7 1PA**        **Lat N53:38:52**        **Long W02:40:06**

## Road Directions

From the M6, Junction 28: Turn right at the bottom of the slip road and remain in the right hand lane in order to turn right onto the A49 towards Euxton. Keep going along this road for about 2 miles, passing under the railway, and you will come to two mini-roundabouts with the Euxton Mills pub on the right at the second. Continue straight on and the road dips over a stone bridge across a river. Take the next left after this bridge into German Lane, after the 'Welcome to Charnock Richard' sign. When the road forks bear left under the railway bridges and follow the lane to the right, parallel with the railway. After another 400 yards the road splits again with a gate to a disused quarry.

Park here, there is room for several cars. The footpath to the first bridge starts opposite this gate, for the second footbridge continue on foot down the lane. It drops steeply down and just as it starts to climb again you will see a small wooden footbridge on the right which is the start of the footpath.

3) Viewed from the southern bridge, 86259 heads the 'Les Ross Daytripper' south towards Birmingham New Street.
*March, 13:15, 40mm*

# Farington Junction

## Location Notes

A footpath, within a field, parallel to the main line just to the south of the junction with the Blackburn Route.

1) 60099 heads north, on the slow lines, with an Enterprise working bound for Blackburn.
*May, 07:30, 115mm*

## Public Transport

Fishwick's, service 111, operates every 10 minutes along Brownedge Road ( A5083) and passes both Leyland and Preston railway stations.

## Amenities

There is nothing at the location, however there are pubs and a Sainsburys Supermarket near the end of the M65. There are also plenty of shops in Leyland Town Centre which is about a 5 minute drive away.

## Accommodation

There is a Premier Inn located on Lostock Lane at the end of the M65.

## Photographic Notes

Early on, before about 08:00, the light will suit northbound trains and from then, until around midday, for southbound. In the summer months

2) 70006 joins the WCML from the Blackburn line.
*May, 11:15, 65mm*

there is also an evening angle available from the bridge looking down on the slow lines.

The line is four track with two fast lines on the eastern side and the slow lines on the western side.

With the exception of local Northern services on the slow and Virgin on the fast it is pot luck as to which lines trains will use.

There is no significant noise from traffic so audio recordings should not be greatly affected.

Later in the summer long trackside grass can become a nuisance. The line is on a slight embankment separated by palisade fencing so a step ladder will normally be required.

# Farington Junction

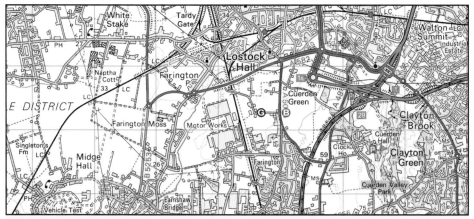

**Postcode: PR25 3RJ**         **Lat N53:42:42**         **Long W02:41:35**

## Road Directions

From the end of the M65 near Preston (Junction 1a) which is a short distance from both the M6 (J29) and M61 (J9), turn left onto the A582, signposted Leyland, for about ¼ mile to the next roundabout then turn left onto the B5254, signposted Leyland. Turn right after a further ¼ mile into Fowler Lane; this is immediately before the road speed reduces to 30mph, and follow the lane to the bridge.

The road is a dead end so there is very little traffic and parking on the lane is no problem. The footpath leads through the farm gate on the east side of the bridge and alongside the fence.

3) 33025 heads a short rake of ECS south on the up fast while heading for Tysley before a charter working.
*May, 09:00, 115mm*

# Bee Lane, Penwortham

## Location Notes
This is a quiet road bridge just off a main road. Little traffic uses it and the bridge is fairly wide.

1) 37059 top & tails with 37069 on a southbound Serco test train bound for Crewe and then Euston.
*August, 15:00, 135mm*

## Public Transport
Fishwicks, service 111, operates every 10 minutes along Leyland Road from Preston railway station and passes the end of Bee Lane.

## Amenities
There are no amenities near to the bridge. However, Lostock Hall is 5 minutes away and has pubs, convenience shops and take-aways.

## Accommodation
The nearest large hotel is the Premier Inn at Bamber Bridge at the end of the M65.

## Photographic Notes
The line here is in a cutting. The main shot is looking north for southbound trains, the sun will be head on around midday. The sides of the bridge vary in height so a step ladder may be an advantage. The line is electrified but the catenary is not too obtrusive and with care, clear shots of engines can be had on both fast and slow lines, although the difficulty is knowing on which line a train will come. Farington Curve Junction is below the bridge however, so trains heading for Blackburn or Ormskirk will be on the left hand lines. Just to the north of the bridge, on the southbound lines, are some signals which will require a lens of at least 70mm to get 'past'.

Whilst there is little traffic on Bee Lane itself, traffic on nearby Leyland Road will be heard on videos.

2) 221127 passes the Ormskirk and Blackburn lines.
*May, 14:00, 155mm*

# Bee Lane, Penwortham

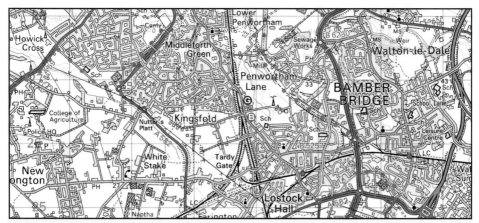

**Postcode: PR1 9SY**          **Lat N53:43:57**          **Long W02:42:09**

## Road Directions

From the end of the M65 (Junction 1a) turn left onto the A582, signposted Lytham St. Annes, and at the next roundabout turn right on the B5254 towards Lostock Hall. You will pass Lostock Hall station on the right then go through three sets of traffic lights in Lostock Hall village. Continue until you come to a roundabout, with a 'Welcome to Penwortham' sign, and turn left into Bee Lane where you will find yourself immediately on the bridge. Parking is possible on the bridge but leave room for traffic to pass.

3) 60163, with 67005 on the back, steams south with the Royal Train, Manchester-bound to collect the Prince of Wales. *February, 15:15, 130mm*

# Brock Level Crossing

## Location Notes

A quiet foot crossing located in between the A6 and M6 roads and adjacent to a Land Rover dealership. There are two places from which you can photograph: by the crossing itself or from a small footbridge over a river 50 yards to the south.

There is not much in the way of shelter here but it won't be far to walk back to the car.

1) Taken from the river bridge, with the car dealership on the left, 185141 heads south over the crossing.
*June, 11:00, 115mm*

## Public Transport

Stagecoach, services 40/41, operate every 30 minutes from Preston to Lancaster along the A6 and stop near the Land Rover garage.

## Amenities

The nearest amenities are in Bilsborrow village ½ mile to the south on the A6. There are several pubs, a shop and a chip shop.

## Accommodation

Old Nells Tavern/Guys Thatched Hamlet in Billsborrow not only has a good pub and restaurant but also reasonably priced accommodation. There is also a Premier Inn nearby.

## Photographic Notes

The location here is best for morning southbound workings. You can take pictures using a variety of lens lengths from either the crossing or along the hedge which is at right angles to the line.

2) 92002 heads north with a driver training trip.
*September, 10:15, 115mm*

Depending on the time of year and whether the farmer has pruned the hedge, a step ladder may be needed. The shot from the footbridge over the river is better for northbound trains, though this will be more into the light.

Noise from the nearby M6 will be intrusive on video recordings.

# Brock Level Crossing

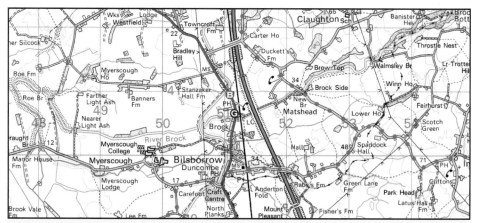

**Postcode: PR3 0RB**               **Lat N53:51:25**               **Long W02:44:31**

## Road Directions

From M6, Junction 32: Take the M55, turning off after about ½ mile onto the A6, head north towards Garstang. You will pass through Broughton traffic lights after just under a mile, then after about another three miles you will reach Bilsborrow Village. About ½ mile further on you will see the Land Rover dealership on the right.

The foot crossing is at the back of the showroom car park and is visible from the main road.

However, it is not advisable to park in the dealership car park. A little further on is a roundabout where you can turn round and park on the pavement outside the showroom. Alternatively, turn left at the roundabout, there is a new garden centre with a large car park.

3) 86101 heads south to Crewe with the electric leg of Compass Tours' 'Ynys Mon Express' charter to Holyhead.
*March, 08:15, 80mm*

# Brock Footbridge

## Location Notes

Probably the best location on this section of the line for afternoon photography, it is a footpath leading across a field to a footbridge.

It is very quiet and the path rarely sees use other than with photographers. As it is an open field there is little shelter.

1) 40145 heads north to Heysham with the 'Buxton Forester' railtour from Birmingham International.
*September, 17:30, 90mm*

## Public Transport

Stagecoach, services 40/41, operate every 30 minutes from Preston to Lancaster along the A6. You will need to alight near the Land Rover dealership in Brock.

## Amenities

The nearest amenities are in Bilsborrow village ½ mile to the south on the A6. There are several pubs, a shop and a chippy.

## Accommodation

Old Nells Tavern/Guys Thatched Hamlet in Billsborrow not only has a good pub and restaurant but also reasonably priced accommodation. There is a Premier Inn nearby too.

## Photographic Notes

Shots can be had at any time of day. In the early morning for northbound trains there is a choice of the railway footbridge, the field or the motorway

2) 20304 and 303 head an early morning flask north.
*August, 08:15, 115mm*

footbridge steps. Once the sun progresses round you have options from either side of the line from the fields. By late afternoon in summer the sun will move round enough for northbound shots. Generally the sun is head on around midday.

In the summer a step ladder may be useful when the lineside vegetation grows. After heavy rain the field will become muddy, so stout shoes may be handy.

The nearby M6 will cause audio problems for videographers, but there is plenty of room for tripods.

# Brock Footbridge

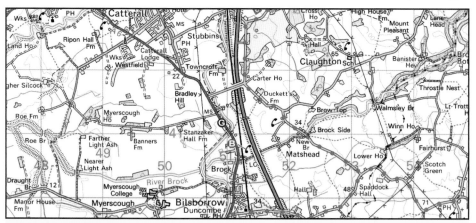

**Postcode: PR3 0RA**       **Lat N53:51:54**       **Long W02:44:38**

## Road Directions

From M6, Junction 32: Take the M55, turning off after about ½ mile onto the A6 and head north towards Garstang Village.

You will pass through Broughton traffic lights after just under a mile then after about a further 3 miles through Bilsborrow Village. About ½ mile further on you will come to a new roundabout. Turning left here leads to a garden centre with a large car park (though please check closing times). Alternatively just after the roundabout there is a canal bridge and about 400 yards further on is a lay-by.

Access to the field is via the farmyard on the southern side of the canal bridge near to the new roundabout. There is a metal gate, muddy fields, and a stile to negotiate to reach the location..

3) 60091 heads south, under the foot bridge, with an engineers track panel working from Carlisle.
*April, 16:00, 80mm*

# Woodacre

## Location Notes

There are two modern footbridges spanning the railway about ¼ mile apart. The northern one, #1, is next to a small factory which strips cable; the southern, #2, one is in fields. Both are also next to the M6 motorway which is parallel to the railway along this section.

1) Colas Rail's 66843 heads south past the northern bridge #1 with the Carlisle-Chirk logs.
*March, 16:15, 80mm*

## Public Transport

Stagecoach, services 40/41, operate along the A6 every 30 minutes between Preston and Lancaster and stop at the top of Gubberford Lane.
It would be about a 25 minute walk to the north bridge and around 30 minutes to the southerly one.

## Amenities

There are none in the area. Garstang is several miles away with plenty of shops and pubs.

## Accommodation

The Crofters Hotel is about a mile away on the A6.

## Photographic Notes

Both bridges are primarily suitable for southbound trains with the sun head on around midday.
Bridge #1 can be used both in the morning and afternoon. Bridge #2 is better suited to afternoon shots. However once the sun has moved round in late afternoon a wide angle northbound shot can also be had from the southern bridge.
Video will be spoiled by the background noise from the M6 and noise from the factory by the northern bridge.

2) At bridge #2, 37194 heads north.
*March, 16:30, 115mm*

3) At bridge #1, a Grant Rail Tamper heads south.
*February, 10:00, 100mm*

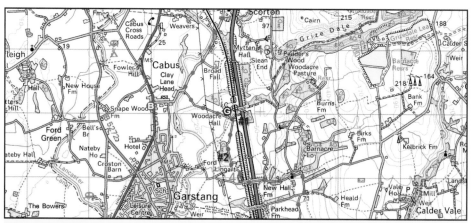

**Postcode: PR3 1DG**                    **Lat N53:54:59**                    **Long W02:45:27**

## Road Directions

From the M6, Junction 33: Take the A6 south towards Garstang. After about 4 miles look out for Snape Wood Lane on the right and the speed camera on the right. Take the next turning left into Gubberford Lane, signposted Scorton. Follow the road round the corner and over the single track bridge then turn immediately right into Hazelhead Lane. After ¼ mile you will see the first bridge in front of you, park where the road widens in front of the factory taking care to leave access room for lorries.

To reach the second bridge continue along the lane, round an 'S' bend. As you approach a farm on the left there is a small gap in the hedge on the left, directly opposite the footbridge. This is the start of the footpath. It is recommended you turn at the farm entrance before parking. There is space on the verge facing back the way you have just come which is slightly wider, so parking is safer on that side.

4) From the southern bridge, #2, 57012 speeds south with the logs, totally ignoring the police speed checks.
*September, 16:15, 145mm*

# Sefton and West Lancashire

## General Notes

This section covers three passenger lines which cross West Lancashire and includes part of the Merseyrail network along the coastal strip of Southport.

The Ormskirk to Preston line is single track with one passing loop at Rufford. At Ormskirk it meets head on with a branch of Merseyrail's Northern Line. However, there is no physical connection between the two. The line from Wigan to Southport is double track along its length. A weight restriction on a bridge towards the Wigan end has led to a nominal ban on loco hauled trains, however these can, and have, run with permission from the Area Chief Engineer. There is also a special dispensation for engineering trains.

The Southport branch of the Merseyrail network is the only one of the three northern lines that is likely to see charter trains as it has a connection with the line to Liverpool Docks. Through trains could run to Ormskirk and Kirkby, joining at Hunts Cross south of Liverpool, but the steep bank out of the central Liverpool tunnel means this does not normally happen.

1) 153301 heads towards Ormskirk from Preston.
*May, 09:15, 60mm*

## Passenger traffic

The Ormskirk line is usually worked by a single class 153 unit spending the day shuttling to and from Preston about every 90 minutes.

The Southport to Wigan line has a much more frequent service with two trains per hour, one from Manchester Airport and one from Manchester Victoria. These are worked by a mix of Northern's class 142, 150 and 156 units. Merseyrail has a fleet of about 60 class 507 and 508 units which externally are virtually identical. These were heavily refurbished in 2004-5 but there are aspirations for the replacement of the fleet soon. The service is intensive with a 15 minute frequency between Liverpool and Southport.

2) DR98910 cleans the leafy line to Southport.
*December, 13:15, 150mm*

## Freight Traffic

There are no regular freight workings on any of these lines. Engineering trains can be seen during line closures, in the past, usually worked by DB Schenker class 66s.

## Occasional Traffic

Autumn months will see daily trips by Network Rail's Multi Purpose Vehicles laying sandite on the Merseyrail lines or jetting on the Wigan line.

Charter trains on the Southport to Wigan line have been less frequent over recent years due to the mentioned bridge restriction, however a couple did run during 2009.

3) 58009 returns from Ormskirk towards Preston.
*December, 14:45, 75mm*

The Ormskirk to Preston line has seen special workings in conjunction with horse racing at Aintree, the Southport Flower Show and the Open Golf Tournament at Royal Birkdale. These are loco hauled top and tailed as there are no run round facilities at Ormskirk.

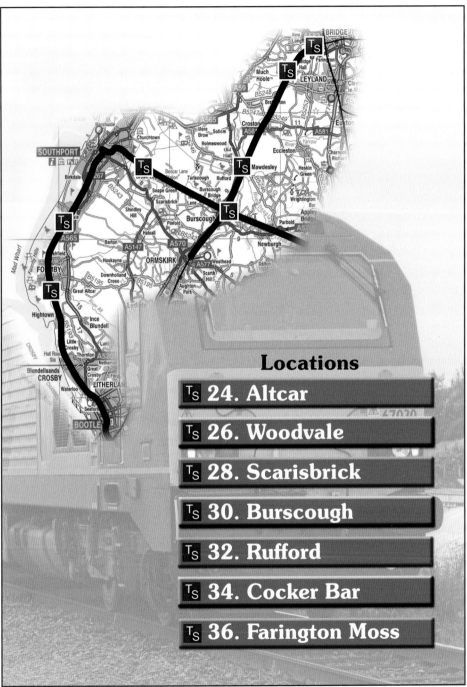

## Locations

- <sup>T</sup>S **24. Altcar**
- <sup>T</sup>S **26. Woodvale**
- <sup>T</sup>S **28. Scarisbrick**
- <sup>T</sup>S **30. Burscough**
- <sup>T</sup>S **32. Rufford**
- <sup>T</sup>S **34. Cocker Bar**
- <sup>T</sup>S **36. Farington Moss**

# Altcar

## Location Notes

A quiet foot crossing over Merseyrail's Southport line on the edge of the town of Formby. The location is popular with dog walkers accessing the nearby dunes and Raven Meols Hills to the west.

1) 508124 passes the 10 mile post while heading south towards Liverpool.
*April, 13:00, 250mm*

## Public Transport

Both Arriva, services 47/48A, and Stagecoach, service X2, run frequently to the end of Altcar Lane from Whitechapel in Liverpool City Centre, which is a few minutes walk from Lime Street Station. You will need to ask for 'The Lighthouse' bus stop.

Formby station, which would be about a 20 minute walk away, is served by Merseyrail services from Liverpool City Centre to Stockport.

## Amenities

Whilst there are none near the location, there is a range of shops in Formby town centre about a mile away. There is also a large Tesco on the A565.

## Photographic Notes

The line runs almost north to south at this point so the light will favour southbound trains for most of the day. In late afternoon the sun should move round enough to be on the front of northbound trains. Photographs can be taken from the foot crossing during both the morning and afternoon with the sun being head on late morning. For afternoon shots you will need to stand on the track side of the access

2) 508115, Southport-bound, passes the foot crossing.
*March, 14:15, 40mm*

gate. More side on shots can also be had from the footpath to the west. As the traffic is usually units, this is probably the most favourable position for northbound trains.

Long grass, especially in summer, will hinder the shot from the crossing looking south.

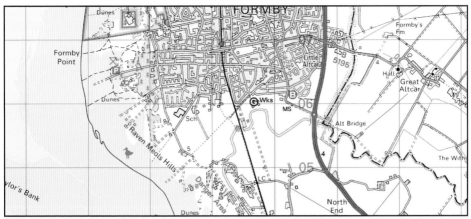

**Postcode: L37 6AN**          **Lat N53:32:42**          **Long W03:04:02**

## Road Directions

If heading from the Southport direction take the A565 towards Liverpool. You will pass RAF Woodvale on the right. Go straight on at the next roundabout, continue through the traffic lights by Tesco, and at the next roundabout turn right (note this will be the third turning signposted Formby). If you are coming along the A565 from the south you will need to turn left here. It will be the first road signposted B5424 Formby. After about 400 yards the road turns to the right, then take the first turning on the left, after the Lighthouse Pub, into Altcar Lane. At the end of the the road turn left into Hogs Hill Lane. Continue down the track, between the 3.5t lorry signs facing you.

The foot crossing is at the bottom of this lane, ahead of you where the lane turns to the left. There is room to park by the access to the old power station.

3) Carrying 'Liverpool capital of culture year' vinyls, 507109 heads towards Southport.
   *April, 13:30, 105mm*

# Woodvale

## Location Notes
Woodvale is a quiet residential suburb to the south of Southport. Out of the three bridges at this location the northernmost one, Kenilworth Road, roughly marks the boundaries of Ainsdale and Woodvale.

1) #2, from the footbridge steps. 507010 accelerates away from a stop at Ainsdale station towards Liverpool.
*April, 11:15, 155mm*

## Public Transport
Ainsdale station is between a 10 and 25 minute walk depending on which of the bridges you are going to. Arriva, services 49/49A, operate every 10 minutes from Southport and cross the Kenilworth Road bridge (#1). Service 49A turns right and is the best option if you wish to get to the Coast Road bridge (#3). You should alight on Pinfold Lane.

2) At bridge #3, 507025 heads south.
*April, 12:45, 135mm*

## Amenities
There is a range of convenience shops and takeaways in Ainsdale village near the station.

## Photographic Notes
There are three bridges across the line in about ¼ of a mile. From the north to south these are #1 Kenilworth Road bridge, #2 a quiet footbridge, and the #3 Coastal Road. The light is usually best for southbound trains with the sun being head on around midday.

3) At bridge #2, 507028 heads north.
*March, 10:45, 325mm*

Kenilworth Road and the footbridge both offer views in either direction, the Coastal Road bridge only has a footpath on one side, due to its width, and so is only really suitable for southbound trains. The bridge parapet here is quite high so a step ladder may be required.

For videoing obviously the two road bridges will suffer from traffic noise. The footbridge will be quieter, however if using a tripod it is worth noting it has a tendency to vibrate when someone is crossing.

# Woodvale

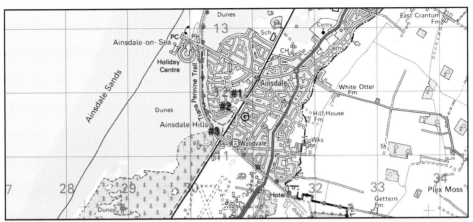

**Postcode: PR8 3TT**  **Lat N53:35:49**  **Long W03:02:52**

## Road Directions

From Southport town centre take the A565 towards Liverpool. Pass Hillside station and fork right at the next roundabout. Pass a cemetery on the left before coming to another roundabout at the top of Ainsdale village. Go straight over the roundabout, second exit, past a Citroen garage and turn right at next set of traffic lights into Kenilworth Road. The road is wide enough to park before the bridge.

For the second bridge, take the second left turn on Kenilworth Road. This is Gleneagles Drive. Turn down here and then first right into Longcliffe Drive. At the end turn left, down Easedale Drive, and there is an entrance to a small car park by the footbridge 250 yards on the right.

For the third bridge, continue on Kendal Way, park at the end of this road, before you reach Coastal Road. From the south on the A565 turn left onto Coastal Road, just after RAF Woodvale. Kendal Way is on the right just before the bridge.

4) At bridge #1, 507009 heads into Liverpool.
*April, 11:30, 135mm*

# Scarisbrick, Pool Hey

## Location Notes
Two quiet level crossings located in flat farm land.

1) With the crossing in the background, 142033 ambles past the stream and heads towards Wigan and then Manchester.
*March, 13:00, 150mm*

## Public Transport
The nearest bus stops are at Carr Cross or at the end of Pool Hey Lane on the main Southport to Ormskirk Road, the A570. It is served by Arriva services 375/385 every 30 minutes. It would be about a 20-25 minute walk to the crossings.

## Amenities
There are none near the location. Southport is 4 miles away and there is a large Tesco and other supermarkets located on the outskirts on the A570.

## Accommodation
Southport has a wide range of Bed and Breakfasts and Hotels.

## Photographic Notes
The line runs east to west therefore the light will be acceptable for most of the day, favouring eastbound

2) 142032 heads east towards Wigan.
*March, 13:30, 80mm*

trains in the morning and westbound in the afternoons. There are two crossings, Pool Hey Lane to the west and Wyke Cop to the east. Pool Hey Lane offers a good close up morning shot of Wigan bound trains however track side equipment spoils the view looking towards Wigan. Wyke Cop has a good lineside afternoon shot looking east but also a pleasing morning shot looking over the drainage ditch towards Pool Hey Lane.

Both locations are quiet though videographers should bear in mind there could be noise from both the barrier crossings and waiting vehicles.

# Scarisbrick, Pool Hey

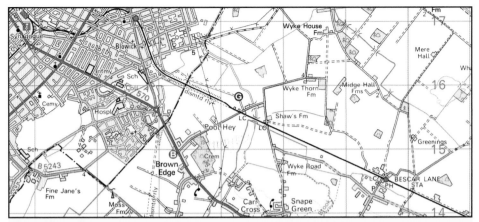

**Postcode: PR9 8AB**　　　　　　　　**Lat N53:37:59**　　　　**Long W02:56:59**

## Road Directions

From the M58, Junction 3: Follow the A570 to Ormskirk passing through the town on the ring road and continue on towards Southport. After about 3 miles you will come to a set of traffic lights by the Morris Dancers pub. Continue straight on and you will pass a church on the left and then come to a left hand bend with a pedestrian crossing before it and a bus stop shelter on right. Turn right at this bend (Carr Cross) into Snape Green. After about ¼ mile turn left into Wyke Cop Road and this will bring you, after about ½ mile, to Wyke Cop AHB crossing. Continue over the crossing for 400 yards and the turning on the left will take you to Pool Hey Lane AHB crossing.

Both lanes are fairly quiet so you should be able to park safely on the verges around the crossings.

3) Approaching the crossing with a Southport-bound working, 142018 catches the last rays of the setting sun.
*December, 15:00, 95mm*

# Burscough, Warpers Moss

## Location Notes

Situated on the Southport to Wigan line, but close to where it passes underneath the Ormskirk to Preston route, this is a rural location on the outskirts of Burscough Village in open flat farmland. A branch of the Leeds to Liverpool canal passes under the railway.

1) From the Leeds and Liverpool canal, 156466 with a Southport-Manchester Victoria working.
*March, 13:15, 80mm*

## Public Transport

Burscough has two stations, Bridge on the Wigan line and Junction on Preston line. Both will be about a 20 minute walk from the location.

## Amenities

The Ship Inn is situated on the canal just to the west and serves food at meal times. There are several pubs and shops in Burscough itself with a Tesco next to Burscough Bridge station.

2) 142038 heads west towards Southport.
*March, 10:45, 170mm*

## Photographic Notes

The line runs east to west and so the sun will be side on around midday and will be best for trains heading towards Wigan in the morning and towards Southport in the afternoon. Pictures can be taken from either the canal or the lane that runs under the railway to the west. Whilst the farmland is open and flat the line is on an embankment in order to cross the canal and road but then dips down to pass under the Preston branch. With a zoom lens it would be possible to take side on shots of traffic on this route across the fields.

Whilst the area is quiet, audio recordings may be affected by cars sounding their horns as they cross the canal bridge.

3) 150276 climbs up from under the Ormskirk line
*April, 12:00, 135mm*

# Burscough, Warpers Moss

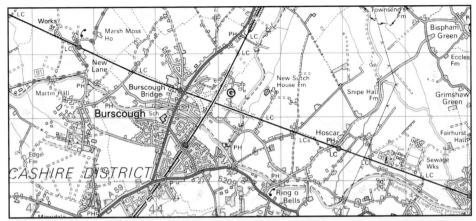

**Postcode: L40 4AJ**                    **Lat N53:36:09**          **Long W02:49:39**

## Road Directions

From the M58, Junction 3: Take the A570 towards Ormskirk for 200 yards and at the next roundabout take the B5240, signposted to Burscough. At the end turn left onto the A577 for 200 yards before turning right to continue on the B5240, signed to Parbold and Burscough. After about 3 miles you come to a mini roundabout. Turn left onto the A5209 and then in 200 yards turn right signposted Hoscar station. Pass the Ring o'Bells pub and cross the canal and take next left into Carr Lane. Continue along here until you come to a narrow canal bridge, with a weak bridge restriction.

There is parking on the lane on the left before the bridge. Alternatively continue over the bridge and next right into Warpers Moss Lane where you will see the railway bridge in front.

4) 150223 with a Southport to Manchester Airport working heads east across a branch of the Leeds & Liverpool canal.
*March, 11:00, 80mm*

# Rufford

## Location Notes
A small village in a rural area with a pub on the main road and the railway at the bottom by a small river.

1) 153351 runs past the marina with an Ormskirk-bound train, viewed from the white marina footbridge.
*February, 15:15, 75mm*

## Public Transport
The station is served about every 90 minutes in each direction by Ormskirk to Preston trains.

## Amenities
The Hesketh Arms is located on the A59 a five minute walk from the station and serves good food at meal times. The local Marina also has a cafe.

## Photographic Notes
The station is located on the only passing loop on the line. A small river flows underneath the railway and there is a small fishing pond next to the line. A footpath runs alongside the river and crosses the line by a foot crossing on the river bridge.

The light is usually best for southbound trains and from about 09:00 to midday the sun will be right for shots of trains crossing the river bridge. There is a shot looking north from the foot crossing in the afternoons, though shadows can be a problem here. The area is rural so is fairly quiet however videographers should bear in mind there could be noise from the barrier crossing and waiting traffic.

There is also a late afternoon side on shot to be had from the white footbridge located in the Marina on the west side of the railway.

2) 153304 heads past the pond towards Ormskirk.
*March, 10:30, 90mm*

3) At the foot crossing, 153304 heads for Ormskirk.
*March, 10:30, 90mm*

# Rufford

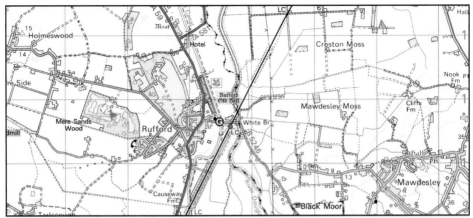

**Postcode: L40 1TB**    **Lat N53:38:08**    **Long W02:48:24**

## Road Directions

Rufford is located on the main A59 trunk route between Liverpool and Preston. Look out for the B5246 towards Parbold which will be on the left if coming from Preston, just after the entrance to Rufford Old Hall or on the right from Liverpool, about 3 miles north of Burscough. The Hesketh Arms is a good landmark from this direction.

The railway station is about 500 yards down this road. There is a station car park on the right just after the crossing, otherwise the Marina's overflow car park is on the left before the railway.

4) Crossing over the canal with a local shuttle service from Preston 153315 heads towards Ormskirk.
*March, 10:00, 55mm*

# Cocker Bar

## Location Notes
Two bridges over the railway with open countryside to the west. The first is a quiet farm track, the second a reasonably busy main road.

1) 153304 heads north towards Preston with the local shuttle service.
*March, 10:45, 80mm*

## Public Transport
Fishwicks, service 111, operates every 10 minutes from Preston, past Leyland station and onto Moss Side. The nearest stop is by the Black Bull pub which is a 10-15 minute walk from the location.

## Amenities
None around the location. There is the Black Bull pub a short distance away towards Leyland. Leyland itself has several large supermarkets and a variety of shops.

## Photographic Notes
The sun will only be on the front in the early morning, or late evening, for northbound trains. Throughout the rest of the day it will favour southbound trains heading towards Ormskirk and will be head on early in the afternoon.

2) Looking north from the southern road bridge.
*April 10:15, 80mm*

The first bridge is quiet and gives good views both directions however the nearby B5248 can be reasonably busy so may impact on videos. The second bridge, on the main road, carries a reasonable amount of traffic. It is safe to stand on the grass verges but may be unsuitable for using tripods. The best view from this bridge is for trains heading towards Ormskirk.

# Cocker Bar

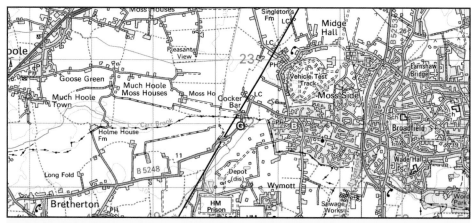

**Postcode: PR26 7TA**          **Lat N53:41:36**          **Long W02:45:12**

## Road Directions

From the end of the M65, Junction 1a: Turn left onto the A582, signposted to Lytham St Annes. Straight on at the next roundabout will take you over the main line. Turn right at the second of the two roundabouts after the bridge, still following signs for Lytham. At the next roundabout turn left onto the B5253 towards Leyland. Go straight on at next roundabout and turn right at next set of traffic lights by the Dunkirk Hall pub onto the B5248 (Dunkirk Lane). Continue past the Black Bull and the road bends sharply to left. There is then an 'S' bend and you will see the lane to the first bridge ahead of you at this second left hand bend. Parking can be a problem, there is none on the lane itself, however the bends on the main road are quite wide so it is possible to park safely on verges if you are careful. Continue on the main road for a further 400 yards and you will see the second bridge. There is a lane on the left just before this bridge on which you can park.

3) Looking north towards Midge Hall. 153332 shuttles between Preston and Ormskirk.
*September, 10:15, 185mm*

# Farington Moss

## Location Notes
A quiet farm crossing in the middle of flat mossland.

1) 153324 ambles towards the crossing with the branch shuttle heading for Preston.
*January, 09:45, 80mm*

## Public Transport
Fishwicks, service 115, operates hourly along Chain House Lane and stops at the end of Parkers Lane.

## Amenities
There is a pub, with a carvery, in New Longton 5 minutes away and there is a range of pubs and shops in Lostock Hall about a mile away.

## Accommodation
There is a Premier Inn near the end of the M65.

## Photographic Notes
Trains heading east towards Preston will have the sun on the front until about 11:00. After this, until mid to late afternoon, it will be best for westbound trains.

There should be little background noise to affect videos.

2) 142035, standing in for the usual Class 153, heads south to Ormskirk.
*April, 09:15, 185mm*

***The location is monitored by cctv as the gates are often left open.***

# Farington Moss

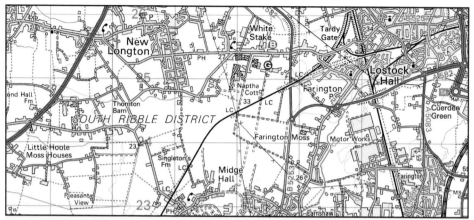

**Postcode: PR4 4JY**      **Lat N53:42:59**      **Long W02:43:23**

## Road Directions

From the end of the M65, Junction 1a, turn left onto the A582, signposted to Lytham St. Annes. Go straight on at the next roundabout which will take you up over the main line. Turn right at the second of the two roundabouts after the bridge, still following signs for Lytham St. Annes. Again turn right at the next roundabout, still on the A582 and pass under the Ormskirk line. Turn left at the traffic lights into Chain House Lane. You will pass Naptha Lane on the left and then, just after the next bus stop on the right, turn left into Parkers Lane. The level crossing is at the end and there is usually room to park before it.

3) 37416 heads the 'Guild and Docker' charter down the Ormskirk branch. 60042 is on the rear of the train.
*November, 15:15, 115mm*

# Manchester to Blackpool

## Passenger Traffic

There is a frequent service over the length of this line operated by Trans Pennine Express and Northern.

Trans Pennine have hourly services from Manchester to Scotland or Barrow-in-Furness and Manchester to Blackpool, each using their 185 units.

Northern uses a variety of second generation units and, currently, three hired in class 180 Adalantes. Services between Manchester and Preston and Manchester and Wigan generally both run half hourly and use class 142, 150 and 156 units. Between Preston and Blackpool there are additionally services from Liverpool using class 156s, York using class 158s and Colne using 142s.

The DFT have recently announced plans to extend the electrification of the West Coast Main line to Blackpool North by 2014.

## Freight Traffic

There is no regular freight traffic booked along the route.

## Occasional Traffic

The main source of any additional traffic is charter trains, often operated by the West Coast Rail company and by the Northern Belle, though any operator may appear. The Blackpool branch rarely sees loco hauled trains although this can occasionally happen and there are often steam hauled specials heading for the Blackpool Illuminations in the late Autumn.

Diversions from the West Coast Main Line can sometimes see Virgin trains use the route via Chorley, both Pendolinos dragged by class 57s and Voyagers.

South of Preston diverted freight will occasionally use the line to Manchester if there are problems, or engineering works, on the West Coast Main Line.

1) 185102 takes holidaymakers to Manchester Airport.
*March, 10:15, 325mm*

2) 66551 and a wagon move through Horwich.
*September, 12:00, 135mm*

3) Dragging 390041 through Euxton, 57304 heads for Preston.
*October, 16:30, 100mm*

## Locations

# Lostock, Lady Bridge Lane

## Location Notes

Lady Bridge Lane has a wide bridge, now carrying just a footpath, across the railway and a small river on the edge of Bolton. It is popular with dog walkers and joggers.

About ¼ mile to the east along a footpath is another similar bridge near the cemetery.

1) At bridge #1, 150141 heads east past the golf course with a Wigan to Rochdale working.
*March, 10:00, 80mm*

## Public Transport

There are two service 575s, operated by First Bus and Arriva, which run frequently down the main Chorley New Road, and stop at the top of both Lady Bridge Lane and Overdale Drive.

## Amenities

Bolton is about 2 miles away and the Middlebrook Retail Park near Horwich is about the same distance. There is a small walker's seated 'picnic area' by the cemetery bridge if you have your own refreshments.

2) At bridge #1, 150268 scoots past.
*March, 15:15, 65mm*

## Photographic Notes

The line runs east to west so the sun will favour eastbound trains towards Bolton and Manchester in the morning and westbound in the afternoon.

At both bridges the best shots are in the morning looking west. There is an east facing shot at Lady Bridge Lane but at the one near Heaton Cemetery large trees create shadows and prevent the best angle. Generally here looking towards Bolton you will have to stand on the wrong side of the railway for the sun. The line is in a wide valley so shadows will normally only be a problem early and late on winter days.

# Lostock, Lady Bridge Lane

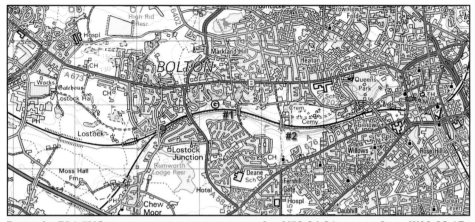

**Postcode: BL1 5NG**          **Lat N53:34:31**          **Long W02:28:17**

## Road Directions

From the M61, Junction 5: Take the A58 towards Bolton. After about a mile the A58 turns left, after a garage, signposted Bury. You cross the valley on a large wide green bridge and at the end turn right onto the A673 towards the Town Centre. Lady Bridge Lane is on the right after ¼ mile. It is the road after Heaton Court Gardens and has a sign on the corner for NHS Ladybridge Hall.

There is room to park at the bottom of the lane by the bridge.

Continuing for a further ¼ mile after Lady Bridge Lane, Overdale Drive is on the right signposted to Overdale Crematorium. It is the road that looks like just an entry to a building immediately after Heaton Grange Gardens. Continue straight down past the Crematorium and park before you reach the Agricultural Centre. Continue on foot down the lane to the bridge.

3) At bridge #2, 57301 drags 390038 east towards Manchester with a diverted London train.
*September, 10:30, 65mm*

# Hart Common

## Location Notes

A small unmade road in farmland crossing two bridges about 500 yards apart. One bridge is on the line that branches off the Manchester to Blackpool route at Lostock Junction taking trains to Wigan, the other is on the old Lancashire and Yorkshire main line from Manchester to Wigan via Atherton which is now reduced to a half hourly service normally operated by class 142s. Crow Nest Junction, where the two routes merge, is ¼ mile to the west on the Wigan side of the location.

## Public Transport

Maytree Travel, service 559, operates hourly between Bolton Moor Lane Bus Station and Hindley and passes the end of the lane.
First Bus, service 32, operates every 30 minutes between Wigan Bus Station and Manchester and stops in Sandy Lane, Hindley, which is about a 10 minute walk away.

## Amenities

There are none at the location. There are several supermarkets in Westhoughton and various local shops both there and in Hindley.

## Photographic Notes

The first bridge you come to spans the Atherton route. This line used to be four track, but was rationalised, with the current two tracks roughly in the middle of the formation.
The line is in a shallow tree-lined cutting so shadows can be a problem. It runs east to west so the sun will be side on around midday. The bridge parapet is quite high so a step ladder will be useful.
The second bridge is about 500 yards away down an unmade road. This is a much lower bridge spanning a two track line. To the east there is also a shallow tree-lined cutting and although it looks west to the junction it is far more open. Light will be best for eastbound (to Bolton) trains until 11:00 after which it will favour trains heading for Wigan. Again in this direction shadows can be more of a problem.
Whilst the nearby main road will create noise to affect videoing at the first bridge, the second bridge is significantly quieter.

1) At bridge #2, 142039 heads east.
*March, 11:00, 200mm*

2) At bridge #2, 142049 heads west to Rochdale.
*March, 11:00, 80mm*

3) At bridge #1, a 142 heads east to Kirby.
*March, 11:45, 280mm*

# Hart Common

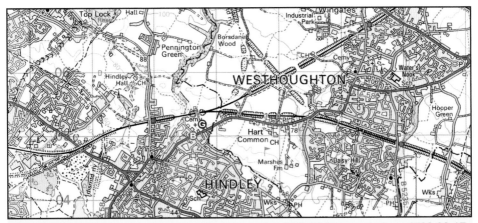

**Postcode: BL5 2DE**          **Lat N53:32:36**          **Long W02:33:17**

## Road Directions

From the M61, Junction 5: Follow the A58 for Wigan. Continue along here for about two miles into Westhoughton. The A58 turns left at the traffic lights just after Sainsburys. You will cross the railway by another set of traffic lights and then enter Hart Common. There is a golf club on the left and shortly after that you will see a row of red brick houses on the right. Jacks Lane is immediately before these on the right. The first bridge is just off the main road so park by the houses as the lane becomes pot-holed after the bridge. It will probably be best to continue on foot down Jacks Lane to reach the second bridge.

4) At bridge #1, 150207 takes the Atherton line with a Kirby to Manchester Victoria working.
*March, 11:15, 325mm*

# Lostock, Lostock Hall

## Location Notes
A long modern footbridge carrying a little used footpath across the railway. It is in open country and surrounded on each side by very wet boggy fields. Stout shoes or wellingtons are required.

1) 57305 drags 390026 on a diverted Virgin West Coast Northampton to Preston working.
*February, 14:00, 80mm*

## Public Transport
Horwich Parkway station is about a 25-30 minute walk from the location. First Bus and Arriva, services 575, run frequently from Bolton and stop on Chorley New Road at the top of Ox Hey Lane.

## Amenities
Middlebrook Retail Park is about ½ mile away and has a wide range of supermarkets and shops and fast food outlets.

## Accommodation
There is a Premier Inn on the retail park by the Reebok Stadium.

## Photographic Notes
Shots can be had from both sides of the line but the light will usually favour standing on the southern end of the bridge. Light will be best for eastbound trains towards Bolton in the morning until early afternoon after which it is best for westbound workings.

2) A 175 heads south to Manchester against the setting sun.
*December, 14:30, 275mm*

The footbridge sides are fairly tall, at about 5 feet, so smaller people may find a step ladder useful. The area around the railway is open and in a very wide flat valley so shadows are not a problem here.

There should be no noise, except for a little from the nearby farm, to affect videos.

# Lostock, Lostock Hall

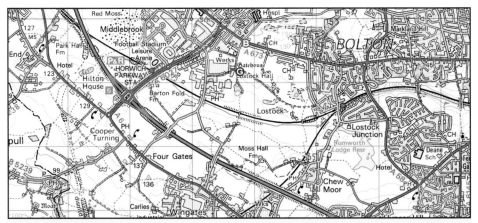

**Postcode: BL6 4AD**          **Lat N53:34:20**          **Long W02:31:07**

## Road Directions

From the M61, Junction 6: Follow the A6027 towards Horwich passing the Reebok stadium on the left. Turn right at the roundabout at the end of the road onto the A673 towards Bolton. After about 400 yards the road climbs slightly and bends gently to the left. Just before this, on the right, is a small turning. Turn into this, Ox Hey Lane, (it is opposite Fall Birch Road) and continue. The lane narrows just after a water works on the right. It is recommended you park here and continue on foot. When you reach a section marked 'Private Road' there is a footpath on the left skirting the garden of a house. Follow this and you will pass through a line of trees then a small wood. Once you are out of this you will see the footbridge below. Generally the right hand side of the field is the driest.

3) 55019 provides passengers with relief from cold turkey on this post-Christmas tour from Derby.
*December, 14:45, 200mm*

# Horwich Parkway

## Location Notes

A small footbridge over the line immediately to the west of Horwich Parkway station. The footpath is little used. Bolton Wanderers football stadium is nearby so the area, though not the footbridge, will be very busy on match days.

1) 43094 heads east with 43098 on a diverted cross-country service to Birmingham.
*November, 13:45, 170mm*

## Public Transport

Horwich Parkway station is well served by trains from Manchester and Preston.

## Amenities

Middlebrook Retail Park is a short walk away with a wide range of shops and fast food outlets.

## Accommodation

There is a Premier Inn next to the Reebok Stadium on the retail park.

## Photographic Notes

The light is best for eastbound trains towards Manchester until early afternoon after which it will favour westbound shots of trains coming through the station. The bridge is quiet, however the M61 motorway is a short distance away so will create background noise on videos.

2) 57309 drags 90021 & 87019 towards Preston.
*September, 14:30, 170mm*

# Horwich Parkway

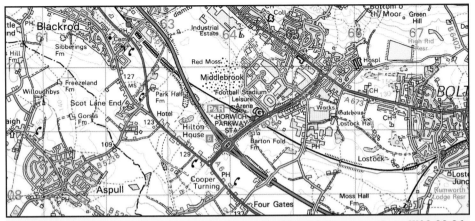

**Postcode: BL6 6LB**      **Lat N53:34:45**      **Long W02:32:36**

## Road Directions

From the M61, Junction 6: Follow the Park and Ride signs onto the A6027 towards Horwich. You cross the railway and turn left at the roundabout before the football stadium onto Burnden Road. First left again will bring you to the station car park. The footpath starts at the western end of the car park, the end farthest away from the station. On weekdays the car park is usually full so you will have to park on the road or a short distance away on the retail park. At weekends there is normally plenty of room to park at the far end near the footbridge, although there could be restrictions for non-rail users on matchdays.

3) Ambling through the Lancashire countryside, 150146 heads south-east towards the Parkway station.
*Photo by Adam Parkinson, April, 12:15, 90mm*

# Heath Charnock

## Location Notes
A quiet foot crossing in the middle of countryside. The area gets very wet after rain so stout shoes or wellingtons are highly recommended.

1) 57315 drags 87012 and a diverted Virgin West Coast MkIII set north towards Preston and approaches the crossing gates.
*March, 14:15, 135mm*

## Public Transport
Stagecoach, services 125/126, operate every 10 minutes between Preston, Chorley and Bolton along the A6.

## Amenities
Chorley Town Centre is 2 miles away with the usual range of shops and take-aways.

## Accommodation
The Chorley South Premier Inn is located close by on the A6.

## Photographic Notes
The best shots here are in the afternoon. From midday onwards the light will favour southbound shots taken from the foot crossing, in late afternoon the sun will move round to favour northbound shots taken

2) 31459 and 602 top and tail a Blackpool Club Train working.
*April, 18:00, 85mm*

from the field. The field is banked and will give you a range of heights from which to shoot. The area is generally quiet and should not provide any problems for videographers.

# Heath Charnock

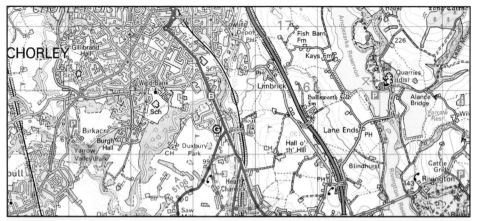

**Postcode: PR7 4AP**               **Lat N53:38:09**               **Long W02:36:38**

## Road Directions

From the M61, Junction 8: Follow the signs for Chorley, A6, and subsequently for signs to 'Town Centre' and then 'Manchester'. Staying on the A6 you will pass a total of 11 roundabouts, passing the railway station on the left (and bus station on right). Morrisons is on the left at roundabout 10. As the A6 leaves town you pass along a straight section with a slight dip. There is a set of traffic lights near the bottom with a road to the right signposted towards Southport and Euxton. After these lights you will see a bus stop on the left with, 50 yards further on, a post in the trees pointing left to the start of the footpath.

Take the next turning on the right into Worcester Place in order to park safely.

Return to the start of the footpath on the main road. This drops steeply into the woods then crosses a bridge over the stream. Follow the path upwards until you are parallel with the canal. After another 100 yards you will come to a bridge over the canal. The footpath continues over this bridge then heads along the edge of field to the foot crossing.

3) 47851 passes the foot crossing with a southbound drag to Crewe.
*October, 12:45, 55mm*

# Buckshaw Village

## Location Notes

This is a large, new, road bridge spanning the railway between a main road and a large development on the land of a demolished ordinance factory.

The bridge itself has wide footpaths and there is no shelter on the bridge itself.

1) High-speed Adelante unit 180103 heads east with a Blackpool North to Manchester Victoria all stations working.
*January, 12:15, 55mm*

## Public Transport

With alternate journeys operated by Stagecoach and Fishwicks, Service 109 crosses the bridge and runs every 30 minutes between Preston, Leyland and Chorley.

## Amenities

There is a new pub located at the other side of the estate. There is a Tesco superstore about 2 miles away on the A581.

## Accommodation

There is a Best Western Hotel at Leyland, just west of Junction 28 of the M6.

## Photographic Notes

The light will be side on around midday. For northbound trains, which will be heading west at this point, shadows should not be a problem even in mid winter. Tall trees do cause shadows looking towards the west but with a standard 50mm lens the first few coaches of trains will be in full sun even during winter. There have been plans to build a new station at this point for several years to serve the new housing, which in future may affect the views, but the recession has probably delayed this. The bridge parapets are just over 5 feet high so a step ladder may be an advantage.

Road traffic noise will cause problems for videographers.

# Buckshaw Village

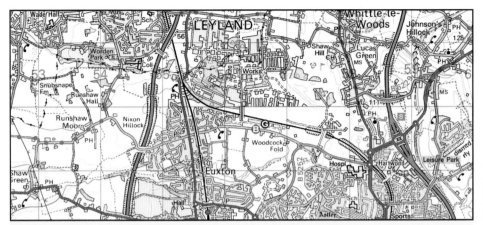

**Postcode: PR7 6AQ**          **Lat N53:40:24**          **Long W02:39:47**

## Road Directions

From the M6, Junction 28: If heading north follow the sign to Chorley B5256 and then after about 300 yards, turn right at the lights onto the A49 towards Euxton. At the next set of lights turn left onto the B5248 for Chorley. Go straight over next roundabout and get in the right hand lane to bear right at the traffic lights by a large statue - 'The Green Man of Buckshaw Village'. You will then find yourself on a long straight road through the new estate which leads directly to the bridge.

Either park on the wide footpaths or turn left at the lights after the bridge, left again at the next set, and double back on yourself along Runshaw College's estate road to a small car park at the foot of the bridge. From the M61, Junction 8: Follow signs for Southport A565. Turn turn left at next roundabout and right at another immediately afterwards. Passing the hospital on the left at the next roundabout turn right towards Euxton, signposted for a low bridge. Either turn right at next set of lights into the college or right at the second set of lights onto the bridge.

2) 57301 provides the power for a diverted Milton Keynes to Glasgow working. 390034 provides the seats.
*October, 15:30, 80mm*

# Lea

## Location Notes

This location is a bridge on a quiet lane across the railway in open countryside on the outskirts of Preston.

1) As 158794 turns off towards Blackpool from Selby, 156427 heads to Manchester Victoria in the background.
*January, 10:45, 150mm*

## Public Transport

Stagecoach, service 88C, operates every 15 minutes from outside Preston station.
Alight near the Cotty Brook pub and walk forward past the pub and under the railway. A footpath then leads alongside the railway to the left just after the bridge and takes you to the location.

## Amenities

There is a Tesco Metro on the main road in Lea. In Cottam, on Hoyles Lane, there is a newsagents and general store.

2) 31602 & 459 head for the bright lights of Blackpool.
*May, 18:30, 130mm*

## Accommodation

There is a selection of hotels in Preston City Centre.

## Photographic Notes

The line is roughly east to west at this point so the sun will be side on at about lunchtime. There are shots both ways but there are some very tall conifer trees creating shadows on the west side of the bridge so a zoom lens will be needed. A step ladder is useful, but not essential, for views to the east due to small bushes by the line side. The field gate can be used if necessary to gain height.

3) 180103 on a crew trainer from Wigan to Blackpool.
*November, 13:15, 275mm*

# Lea

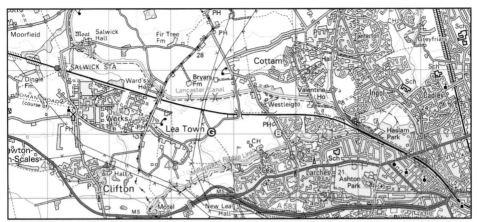

**Postcode: PR4 0RE**                    **Lat N53:46:32**                    **Long W02:46:26**

## Road Directions

From the M6, Junction 32: Take the M55 for a very short distance before turning off, at junction 1, onto the A6. Turn left at the bottom of the slip road, towards Preston, and at the first set of traffic lights turn right onto Lightfoot Lane. After crossing a railway bridge with separate footpath bridges on either sides, take the second right turn, still Lightfoot lane, signposted 'Lightfoot Lane (Part)'. Go straight on at the Stop Junction/crossroads into Hoyles Lane and continue for about a mile to the end. Turn left and at the next bend turn right, going straight on as the road bears left, by the primary school. Follow this lane over the canal and there is room to park on the left opposite the cottages as you approach the railway bridge.

4) Promoting battery power to the Tory Party Conference, hybrid power car 43089 leads the NMT towards Blackpool.
*September, 16:30, 135mm*

# Treales

### Location Notes
A very quiet farm bridge in open fields that forms part of a little used public footpath.

1) 47703 and 712 top & tail the Blue Pullman with a London Euston to Blackpool illuminations charter.
*November, 12:45, 225mm*

### Public Transport
Hegarty Travel, service 77, serves Treales village every 2 hours during the main part of the day from near Preston station, and also passes Kirkham Station.

### Amenities
There is a pub in Treales and also a range of shops 2 miles away in Kirkham.

### Photographic Notes
The sun will be side on to trains around midday so the light is generally best in the morning for trains heading east from Blackpool and in the afternoon heading west from Preston.

You are in quiet farmland so there is unlikely to be too much background noise to disturb videos.

2) 156460 in experimental Northern Colours heads to Blackpool.
*January, 10:30, 135mm*

# Treales

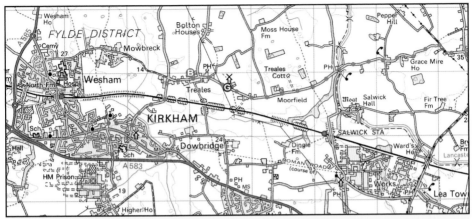

| Postcode: PR4 3UX | Lat N53:47:06 | Long W02:50:23 |
|---|---|---|

## Road Directions

From the M55, Junction 3: Take the A585 south towards Kirkham. At the next roundabout turn left onto the B5192 to Kirkham. If your sat-nav instructs you to turn left into Mowbreck Lane ignore this as it is not a through route. At the mini roundabout, at the end of the road, bear left and then at the second go straight on, continuing past Kirkham station. Turn left at the traffic lights by the St. Georges Hotel and proceed along the main street. Go straight over the next mini roundabout and take the road on the left signposted Inskip and Treales. After about a mile you will cross the railway and enter Treales village. You will pass the Derby Arms on the left then as you leave the village you go under the power lines. After this you will see some trees on the left with a mirror on a pole on the right of the road opposite the entrance to an old windmill. By the mirror is a farm gate, this is the footpath. It is recommended you turn your car round and park on the verge facing the other way just to the west of the gate.

The footpath skirts the left hand edge of the field. Half way down the length of the field there is a stile into the next field on the left. Once you have crossed this you will see the railway bridge at the far side.

3) Heading east, 180108 handles the mid-morning Blackpool to Manchester Victoria Adelante trip.
*January, 11:45, 150mm*

# Kirkham Tip

## Location Notes

A footbridge spanning what used to be two separate routes to Blackpool. In latter days the old main route became used as a spoil tip. Some of the sidings still exist but are not used.

1) 47712 top & tails with 703 on an empty stock movement to Preston after a Euston-Blackpool charter. *November, 13:15, 90mm*

## Public Transport

Stagecoach, service 61, operates every 30 minutes between Preston and Blackpool. The nearest stop will by the Ribby Hall Holiday Village on the B5259.

## Amenities

The nearest are in Kirkham about 2 miles away which has a wide range of shops and pubs.

## Photographic Notes

The line is running roughly east to west at this point. It will be best for westbound trains in an afternoon and eastbound during the morning.

Although the line is in a cutting it is shallow and wide so shadows are not a major problem. The area surrounding the bridge is rural and you are some distance from the nearest road so there is little background noise. The bridge has recently been replaced and as the sides are about 5 feet high now, a step ladder will be an advantage.

2) Exmoor Explorer 158855 with York to Blackpool service. *January, 12:45, 185mm*

# Kirkham Tip

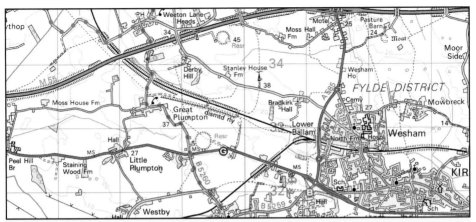

**Postcode: PR4 2RJ**        **Lat N53:47:33**        **Long W02:54:60**

## Road Directions

From the M55, Junction 3: Take the A585 south towards Kirkham. At the second roundabout turn right towards Weeton. After less than half a mile you will see a transmitter aerial in a field on the right. On the left of the road, opposite this, is a parking area. Park here, taking care not to block any of the gates. You will see the footbridge in the distance over the fields, to the right. Walk down the field track and round the fields to reach the footbridge.

3) A Black 5 heads west with an illuminations special to Blackpool from the East Lancashire Railway.
*October, 14:00, 125mm*

# 'Copy Pit Line'

## General Notes

This line was very busy at the end of steam with coal traffic, so when Preston Power Box was built the signalling was extended to include the whole route. However with the closure of several power stations this traffic died away and the line, especially between Burnley and Todmorden, was under threat. The 1980s saw a limited passenger service restored over 'Copy Pit' and this was so popular that today's hourly service was soon introduced. It now provides an important link between East Lancashire and Yorkshire for both passengers and once again, for freight.

1) 158901 with a York to Blackpool North service.
   *December, 13:00, 220mm*

## Passenger Traffic

There are two regular services on this line. One is the hourly Blackpool to York service operated by Northern's class 158 units. The other operates to Colne, branching off from the through route at Burnley, usually utilising class 142s.

## Freight Traffic

The most reliable freight using the whole route is the three times a week bogie oil tank train from Preston Docks to Lindsey Refinery. This runs in the early morning to Preston, normally on Mondays, Wednesdays and Fridays, and departs back from the Docks around 09:00. Freightliner operates coal trains on an as required basis. West of Blackburn sees more trains. There is a weekly service from Warrington to Blackburn conveying Cargowaggons, also several daily services routed from Carlisle via Settle use this route to regain the main line. These include a departmental DB Schenker working, the Colas log train (when it is routed via Appleby), both timed through Blackburn late afternoon, and a GBRF Gypsum service heading the other way. Freightliner operates a northbound ballast train though this is normally at night.

2) 60059 with the Preston tanks at Lostock Hall.
   *August, 14:15, 135mm*

## Occasional Traffic

The line is popular with rail tours, especially with steam-hauled trains due to the severity of the climb to Copy Pit. The Preston to Blackburn section forms part of the diversionary route via Settle to Carlisle when the West Coast Main Line is closed so can see Virgin passenger services, now usually just Voyagers, and other diverted freight trains.

3) 47815 with a Runcorn to Edinburgh charter.
   *June, 08:20, 50mm*

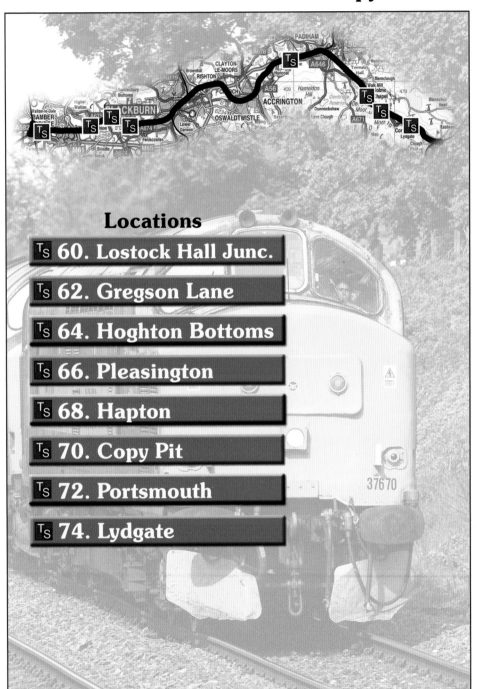

## Locations

60. Lostock Hall Junc.

62. Gregson Lane

64. Hoghton Bottoms

66. Pleasington

68. Hapton

70. Copy Pit

72. Portsmouth

74. Lydgate

# Lostock Hall Junction

## Location Notes

This is a fairly busy road bridge crossing the line at the junction between the main Preston to Blackburn line and the freight only spur heading from the northbound West Coast Main Line.

1) 66205 waits at the branch signal before heading off with the weekly Warrington to Blackburn trip working.
*February, 09:00, 275mm*

## Public Transport

The location is less than a 10 minute walk from Lostock Hall station.

## Amenities

There is a range of shops, pubs and take-aways in Lostock Hall village, just north of the station.
There is a large Sainsburys and several pubs near the end of the M65.

## Accommodation

There is a Premier Inn located on Lostock Lane at the end of the M65.

2) 31128 and 454 with a Birmingham to Preston railtour.
*January, 13:00, 65mm*

## Photographic Notes

The view is more open for a morning shot of eastbound trains coming from the Preston direction.

Trees will cause shadows when the sun is low both for the afternoon shot facing east and for trains coming off the branch from the mainline.

The bridge is not really suitable for videoing due to the traffic, however trains coming from Preston are likely to be working hard due to the gradient. Line speed is relatively low at 40mph on the main line.

# Lostock Hall Junction

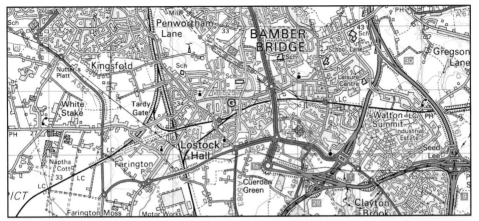

**Postcode: PR5 5XL**       **Lat N53:43:32**       **Long W02:40:57**

## Road Directions

From the end of the M65 Junction 1A: Turn left onto the A582 (signposted Lytham St Annes) and move into the outside lane. It is only about ¼ mile to the next roundabout and before you reach it you will see 'Todd Lane South' on the right hand side of the dual-carriageway.

Use the roundabout to double back and turn left into Todd Lane. About 400 yards up the road you will see the road curve to the right and start climbing to the bridge.

It is best to turn left, before the bridge, into Moss Bridge Park in order to find a safe spot to park your car.

3) 60053 heads east to the Humber Lindsey oil refinery with the thrice-weekly empty tanks from Preston.
*August, 13:30, 115mm*

# Gregson Lane

## Location Notes

One of a series of crossings in a short distance, this one is in open fields. There is the occasional dog walker but few people actually use this foot crossing.

1) 60007 heads west with a Carnforth-Hellifield-Carnforth circular loaded test run before a trip to Yorkshire.
*April, 15:30, 135mm*

## Public Transport

Stagecoach, service 150/151, operate every 30 minutes from Preston Bus Station to Bamber Bridge via Gregson Lane, stopping on Alma Row.

## Amenities

There are several pubs and a a few shops in the village.

## Accommodation

There is a Premier Inn located near the end of the M65 at Bamber Bridge.

## Photographic Notes

The best shots here are either in the morning, of eastbound trains, or in the afternoon for westbound. The sun will be head on towards late afternoon so in summer evenings it will have moved round far enough to shoot westbound trains from the north side of the line.

2) 142066 catches the winter sun en route to Colne.
*November, 09:00, 40mm*

There are open fields on both sides of the line so shadows, even in winter, are not a problem.

The next crossing is a controlled barrier road crossing so while this gives warning of approaching trains, it may interfere with audio sound tracks depending on wind direction.

# Gregson Lane

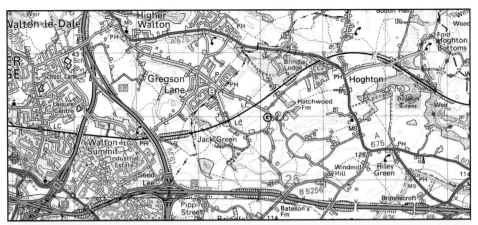

**Postcode: PR5 0DL**        **Lat N53:43:49**        **Long W02:36:33**

### Road Directions

From the M65, Junction 3: Follow the signs for A675 towards Walton-le-Dale. At the next junction fork left, remaining on the A675 and continue for a couple of miles, crossing a bridge over the railway, until you reach Coupe Green. You will pass the Old Oak Inn on the right and just after, as the road bends to the left, turn left into Daub Hall Lane. At the stop sign in Gregson Lane turn left then take the second right into Bournes Row (by the Black Horse pub).The street ends in a mill with a long row of terraced houses on the left. Park by these houses. Just before you enter the mill there is a small unmade track on the left and round the back of the yard the footpath runs to the railway.

Whilst there is a crossing on this track, the better foot crossing is just over the next field to the left.

3) 37401 clags it up at the front of the weekly Blackburn trip from Warrington Arpley.
*April, 09:45, 80mm*

# Hoghton Bottoms

### Location Notes

Two bridges over the railway and a foot crossing. One bridge carries a fairly quiet lane, the other is a farm bridge carrying a little used footpath.

1) Hired in from South West Trains 158888 heads west with a York to Blackpool North Northern working.
*January, 14:30, 80mm*

### Public Transport

Lancashire United, service 152, operates every 30 minutes between Preston and Blackburn and stops at the Boars Head pub on the main road at the end of the lane.

### Amenities

There is the Boars Head pub on the main road, but the nearest convenience store is in Coupe Green about 2 miles away.

### Photographic Notes

The first (western) bridge is the best for morning shots of eastbound trains. These can also be taken from the second bridge which carries the lane however this is really better for trains in the opposite direction in the afternoon or evening, especially since vegetation clearance has taken place. There is a large wooded hill here on the west side of the line so shadows will be a problem in winter.

2) 66168 heads east with the Burngullow to Irving tanks.
*May, 13:15, 115mm*

Just down from the second bridge is a foot crossing which enables shots in both directions.

The bridges are at the top of two uphill sections of line so trains will be working hard in both directions, more so heading east. However, the foot crossing or the western bridge will be better for videoing.

# Hoghton Bottoms

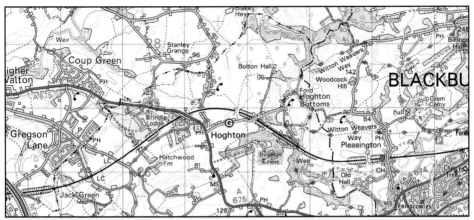

**Postcode: PR5 0RY**                **Lat N53:44:15**                **Long W02:34:48**

## Road Directions

From the M65, Junction 3: Follow the signs for the A675 towards Walton-le-Dale. At the next junction fork left continuing on the A675 for about a mile until you pass the entrance to Hoghton Tower on the right. Just after this you will see the Boars Head pub, with stone bus shelters outside. Immediately before the pub is the lane to Hoghton Bottom, Chapel Lane. As you go down the lane you will see two national speed limit signs. On the left just after these is a public footpath sign pointing across the field to the first bridge, the top of which will be visible. Continuing down the lane will bring you to the second bridge. There is room to park after it, outside the chapel.

A public bridleway leads down to the foot crossing from beside this bridge.

3) Captured from the western bridge, the CFPS's 40145 heads up a West Ruislip to Carlisle charter for Pathfinder.
*April, 11:15, 80mm*

# Pleasington Golf Course

## Location Notes

A farm bridge over the line next to a golf course on a track belonging to the golf club. Please respect that this is private property.

1) 66083 heads west towards Blackburn with the empty Preston Docks to Lindsey tanks.
*Photo by Adam Parkinson, May, 10:15, 130mm*

## Public Transport

Pleasington Station is a 5 minute walk away. Served by trains from Blackburn to Blackpool South.

## Amenities

There is a pub by the station. The nearest large range of shops is 4 miles away in Blackburn.

## Photographic Notes

Shots can now be taken both ways from this bridge following vegetation clearance. In the morning the light will be best for eastbound trains, although the tall conifer trees create shadows. Afternoon shots can be taken of westbound trains leaving the station.

There can be farm type tractors and other equipment passing as the golf course maintenance department is close by but this should not affect video sound tracks too much.

2) A 142 heads east with a Colne working from Blackpool South.
*April, 12:45, 275mm*

# Pleasington Golf Course

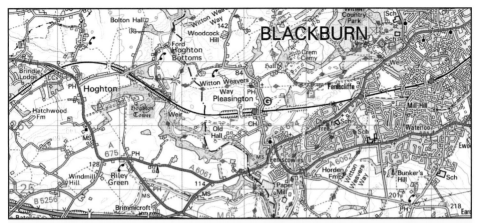

**Postcode: BB2 5JH**        **Lat N53:43:51**        **Long W02:32:53**

## Road Directions

From the M65, Junction 3: Follow signs for the A674 to Blackburn. Turn right at the next traffic lights, continuing on the A674 for about a mile. Look out for a left turn, a brown tourist sign to 'Pleasington Golf course', as you climb the hill into Blackburn. Follow this lane down past the church, across the river and up the other side. As you approach the railway bridge and station there is a small lane on left, opposite the pub, marked 'Private Road'. This lane takes you through the Golf Club outhouses and down to the bridge. It is best to park by the station and walk down the lane to the bridge, although you could continue down the private road and providing you park considerately by the bridge, the ground staff should not mind.

3) 37401 startles the golfers as it clags past with a Blackburn to Warrington Enterprise working.
*Photo by Adam Parkinson, November, 14:00, 145mm*

# Hapton

## Location Notes

This location is near a small station located alongside the M65. There are field shots to the west and east of the station and also a footbridge just to the west that links two areas of housing.
The field is on a little used footpath, the footbridge links two areas of housing but is fairly quiet.

1) 66227 heads east, over the A56 bridge, with the empty tanks from Preston Docks to the Lindsey refinery.
*Photo by Andrew Wills, October, 09:30, 50mm*

## Public Transport

Hapton is served by hourly trains running between Preston and Colne.

## Amenities

Very little in the area; Burnley and Accrington are both about 5 miles away.

## Photographic Notes

The primary morning shot is from a field located about 500 yards west of the station as eastbound trains cross the A56 road bridge. For west bound trains in the afternoon the footpath across a field to the east of the station provides a good view with a telephoto lens. Trains will be climbing here. Telegraph wires in the distance may cause a visual nuisance. The footbridge immediately to the west of the station provides views in either direction though it is better for eastbound workings, shadows will be a problem here in the winter months.

2) Viewed from the footbridge, 158758 heads east to York.
*January, 13:30, 95mm*

For all three viewpoints noise from the M65 will be intrusive on audio sound tracks.

# Hapton

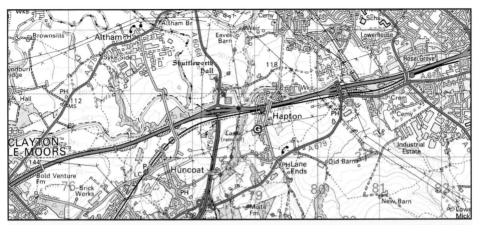

**Postcode: BR11 5RF**              **Lat N53:46:52**              **Long W02:19:27**

## Road Directions

From the M65, Junction 8: Take the A56 south towards Bury for about ½ mile, coming off at the first junction and turning left onto the A679 towards Hapton. After just under ¾ mile turn left on Manchester Road, opposite the Hapton Inn towards the station. The road drops downhill, watch out for a turning on the left signposted to the recreation ground. Turn left here then first right brings you to a car park. The footbridge is just to the left here. To reach the morning shot cross the bridge and turn left onto a footpath alongside the M65. Drop down to the canal and turn left under the bridge. The path climbs up by the railway, cross at the foot crossing and turn right to the next field. The footpath leading to the afternoon shot starts across the road, by the station and leads east down between the houses and the railway.

3) Napier clag fills Lancashire sky as 55019 heads west with the post-Christmas Derby circular tour.
*December, 13:35, 270mm*

# Copy Pit

## Location notes
The bridge, known locally as Windy Bridge, is next to the summit of the line. Set in a deep valley the bridge gives a virtually uninterrupted view in both directions along the line.
It is at the top of the valley linking Yorkshire and Lancashire.

1) 66013 breasts the summit of the line and begins to descend, southbound towards Todmorden and then on to Lindsey. *April, 10:45, 185mm*

## Public Transport
First Bus, services 589/592, and Transdev 'Starship 1' operate every 30 minutes between Burnley and Todmorden and pass the location. However, the Transdev service does not run at peak hours.

## Amenities
None at the location. Todmorden is the nearest town with a range of shops. There are various convenience shops, pubs and chip shops between Copy Pit and Todmorden.

## Accommodation
There are some hotels in the Todmorden/Hebden Bridge area.

## Photographic notes
The light is best for trains heading east towards Yorkshire in the morning and through until just after midday after which it will favour westbound workings. Shots looking west can be taken from the busy road bridge as the train mounts the summit 200 yards away. Shots looking east can be taken from the bridge or from along the wall along the pavement.
Traffic noise will be prominent on videos. This can be a very popular spot and will be busy with enthusiasts when there is a special working due.

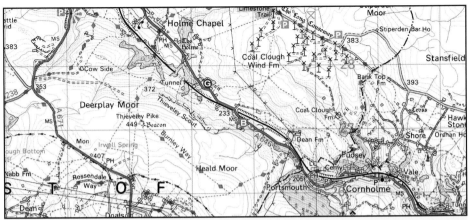

**Postcode: BB10 4TA**     **Lat N53:44:30**     **Long W02:10:22**

## Road directions

From the eastbound only M65, Junction 9: Use junction 8 to change direction if travelling westbound.
Come off the motorway and at the roundabout turn left onto the A679 towards Burnley. Turn right at the
next set of traffic lights, right hand lane, onto the A646 towards Halifax. After about 3 miles you will have to
turn right then immediately left in order to stay on the A646. Pass under the railway and follow the road up
the valley for around 2 miles and you will cross over the railway on the bridge which forms this location.
There is generally room on the verge just before the bridge to park, however, especially when a special
train is due, it may be necessary to use the large lay-by which is on the right about 300 yards after the
bridge. If you are coming from Todmorden, take the A646 towards Burnley out of the town. The lay-by is on
the left around 500 yards after you enter Lancashire and the bridge just after that.

2) After slipping to a stand near the summit, 76079 restarts the 'Cotton Mills Express' to Manchester.
*January, 12:30, 70mm*

# Portsmouth

## Location Notes

This location is a small farm bridge close to the summit of the line at Copy Pit. It is just on the Lancashire side of the county boundary.

1) Coasting downhill with the empty Lindsey tanks, 66086 heads south towards the Humber.
*March, 10:00, 70mm*

## Public Transport

First Bus, services 589 and 592, provide a 30 minute service along the main road between Todmorden and Burnley and pass the location. Transdev 'Starship 1' also operates every 30 minutes although it does not run at peak hours.

If coming from the Yorkshire side it will be cheaper to get off at the last stop before the county boundary.

## Amenities

None in the area. There are various shops and pubs scattered along the main road westbound towards Todmorden.

## Photographic Notes

The best shots are for eastbound trains heading towards Yorkshire and the light is good for this during the latter part of the morning and through to early afternoon. The main road is nearby so there will be some traffic noise on videos.

Eastbound trains will be coasting downhill but westbound trains heading towards Burnley will be working hard towards the summit. The sun will move round to this direction mid to late afternoon.

2) 158907 heads north with a York to Blackpool working.
*January, 12:45, 80mm*

# Portsmouth

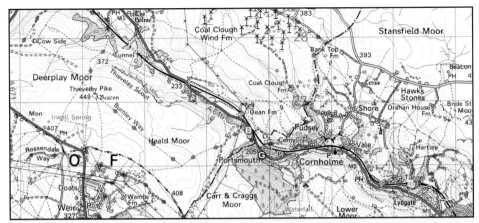

**Postcode: OL14 8PT**          **Lat N53:44:15**          **Long W02:09:36**

## Road Directions

From the M65, Eastbound only Junction 9: Use junction 8 to change direction if travelling westbound. Turn right at the top of the slip road and left at the roundabout onto the A679 towards Burnley. Turn right at the next set of traffic lights onto the A646 towards Halifax. After about 3 miles you will have to turn right then immediately left in order to remain on the A646. Pass under the railway and after a further 2 miles or so you will cross back over the railway. There is a large lay-by on the right hand side and you should then see the two arch bridge over the railway on the left. At the corner by the bridge there is a small entry into a car park belonging to the local angling society located next to the bridge.

If you are coming from the Yorkshire side, take the A646 towards Burnley out of Todmorden. The entrance to the car park is on the bend immediately after the 'Welcome to Lancashire' sign.

3) 60053 descends the bank in the Yorkshire direction with a re-timed lunchtime working of the Preston-Lindsey tanks.
*August, 14:15, 80mm*

# Lydgate

## Location Notes

Lydgate is in a fairly narrow valley just above Todmorden. The line crosses a viaduct and there are views of this and also shots off a small road bridge over the railway. This bridge has recently been rebuilt and with new pallisade fencing so a step ladder will usually be necessary. However, it should be noted that the lane is very steep and narrow so great care will need to be taken when using this.

1) 158797 with a York to Blackpool working just after crossing the viaduct.
*March, 12:45, 115mm*

## Public Transport

First Bus, services 589 (from Rochdale) and 592 (from Halifax), operate every 30 minutes between Todmorden and Burnley and pass the location.

## Amenities

Todmorden is about a mile away and has a market, a supermarket, a range of shops and takeaways.

## Photographic Notes

In the morning the light will be best for eastbound trains. There is a limited shot from the road bridge as trains round a curve in the hillside. After about midday the sun will come round for head on shots of trains coming across the viaduct, again, taken from the bridge.

2) 158794 with a Blackpool to York service.
*March, 09:45, 40mm*

The afternoon is the best time for the preferred shot of westbound trains crossing the Lydgate viaduct. To get these you will need to climb the opposite hillside. It should be noted that a new building has been constructed in the foreground, roughly in the area of trees in picture 3, though this should not impact on the shot too much.

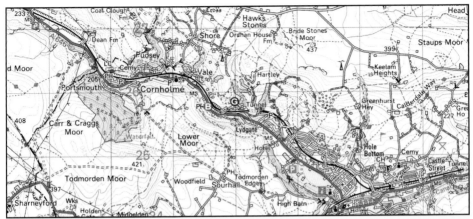

**Postcode: OL14 8AY**          **Lat N53:43:36**          **Long W02:07:28**

## Road Directions

From the M65, Eastbound only Junction 9: Use junction 8 to change direction if travelling westbound. Turn left at the roundabout onto the A679 towards Burnley as far as the next set of traffic lights where a right turn will take you onto the A646 towards Halifax. Continue along this road for 5-6 miles, remaining on the A646. You will cross the railway a total of four times and eventually will pass through Cornholme. As you enter Lydgate the 'Staff of Life inn' is on the left. The next turning on the left, by the bus stop, takes you up to the over bridge. There is room to park before it. Just after this turning there is a small track on the right which will give you access to the hillside. There is nowhere to park on the track, as it is a footpath on a driveway to a house, so you will need to try and park on the pavement on the main road.

If coming from the Yorkshire side, take the A646 towards Burnley out of Todmorden. After a mile you will see Lydgate viaduct on the right. The lane to the bridge, on the right, is marked the Staff of Life car park.

3) 40145 exits the tunnel and crosses the viaduct with the Bradford to Morecambe leg of the 'Buxton Forester' charter.
*September, 15:45, 55mm*

# Bolton to Hellifield

## General Description

This is a secondary route in two parts. Between Bolton and Blackburn the line is largely single track with a loop at Darwen. It climbs steeply to a summit just north of Entwistle where it passes through a long tunnel. After Blackburn the line is double track throughout. Once past Clitheroe the line is usually used only by freight except in summer and for diversions.

## Passenger Traffic

There is an hourly all stations local service along the line from Manchester to Clitheroe. This is exclusively worked by Northern's class 150 units.

On summer Sundays their class 156 units can be seen north of Blackburn on the 'Dalesrail' service to Carlisle.

## Freight Traffic

No freight is booked over the section of line between Bolton and Blackburn. Beyond Blackburn the line is used by trains coming off the Settle and Carlisle line. There is a daily southbound DB Schenker departmental train in the afternoons and the Colas log Train has also started running this way. Northbound there is a GBRf gypsum train from Fiddlers Ferry to Newbiggin and a Freightliner ballast train, though this usually runs at night. Freightliner coal trains can also run this way on an as required basis occasionally producing a class 70.

A three times weekly train serves the Cement Works at Clitheroe. This usually runs late in the morning on Monday, Wednesday and Friday south from Hellifield to Horrocksford Junction where the works are situated, returning in the early evening.

## Occasional Traffic

North of Blackburn the line forms part of a diversionary route when the West Coast Main Line is closed. On these occasions Virgin's Voyagers and Pendolinos (the latter dragged by class 57s) can be seen. In addition this may mean additional freight services.

A regular steam hauled rail tour is the 'Cotton Mill Express'. This takes a circular route from Manchester and usually returns south from Blackburn to Bolton via this line.

1) 150218 heads to Blackburn from Clitheroe.
   *January, 15:45, 75mm*

2) 60096 with a Carlisle to Crewe working at Hellifield.
   *Photo by Denis Bradley, April, 15:00, 115mm*

3) 57302 drags 390043 through Lamb Roe.
   *Febuary, 14:15, 90mm*

# Bolton to Hellifield

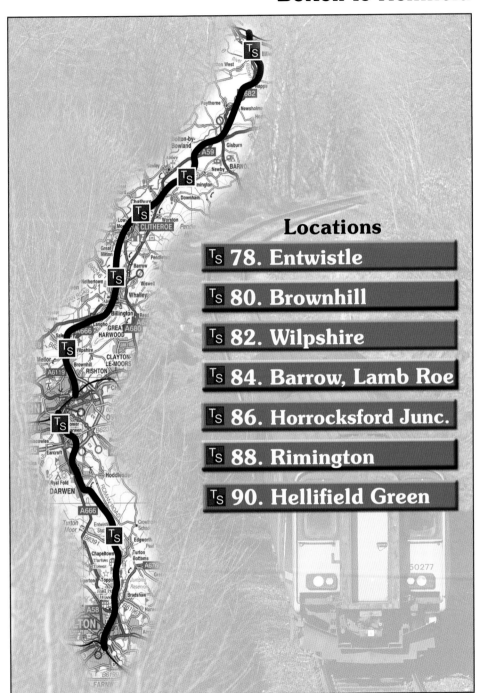

## Locations

**T S** **78. Entwistle**

**T S** **80. Brownhill**

**T S** **82. Wilpshire**

**T S** **84. Barrow, Lamb Roe**

**T S** **86. Horrocksford Junc.**

**T S** **88. Rimington**

**T S** **90. Hellifield Green**

# Entwistle Reservoirs

## Location Notes

A country park surrounding several reservoirs on the edge of the West Pennine Moors. The railway crosses here by a tall viaduct. The area is popular with dog walkers. The footpaths can be muddy after wet weather so wellingtons are recommended.

1) Heading north towards Blackburn, Sprinter 150277 enters the cutting under the Green Arms road bridge.
*March, 14:45, 55mm*

## Public Transport

Entwistle Station is a short walk by public footpaths from the location and is served hourly by Manchester to Blackburn trains.

## Amenities

There are none in the area. Edgworth village has several shops and a pub.

## Photographic Notes

There are two locations here. The first is the road bridge carrying the B6391 over the railway to the south of the viaduct. The light will be best for southbound trains for most of the day though the sun will be head on around noon. Shadows can be a problem as the line is in a tree lined cutting, but longer lenses will get you past this. The former double track line is now singled with the remaining track on the western side of

2) Viewed from the western side, 150244 crosses the viaduct.
*March, 14:15, 85mm*

the formation. Northbound shots can now be had from this bridge following vegetation clearance though by the time the sun has moved onto the front, around 16:00, shadows may be a problem.

The second location offers a shot of the viaduct from the causeway on the western side of Wayoh Reservoir. This is best in the morning until about 10:00 although if it is cloudy this shot can be on all day. On this side of the viaduct is a tree lined valley which restricts shots. Currently it is just possible to find gaps in the trees to get a clear shot of the top of the viaduct.

# Entwistle Reservoirs

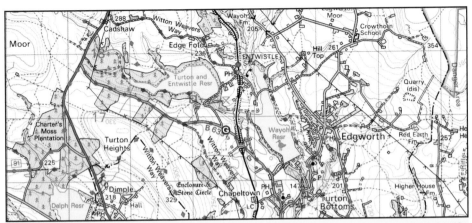

**Postcode: BL7 0NF**        **Lat N53:38:58**        **Long W02:24:53**

## Road Directions

From the M65, Junction 4: Take the A666 towards Darwen, following it round the town centre and staying on the A666 towards Bolton afterwards. Once you leave Darwen look out for a left hand turn after a few miles onto the B6391, signed towards Chapeltown. After passing the entrance, on the left, to Batridge Barn Car Park, take the next left after this into Batridge Road and this will bring you to Entwistle Reservoir. At the rear of the car park on the right a concessionary footpath leads through the woods to the viaduct and Wayoh Reservoir. Continuing past the entrance to Batridge Road, along Green Arms Road, will bring you to the railway bridge. There is room to park in the entrance on the right next to it.

3) 45407 crosses Entwistle viaduct and the Wayoh reservoir, while hauling the 'Cotton Mill Express' to Blackburn.
*Photo by Jack Boskett, December, 10:00, 28mm*

# Brownhill, Blackburn

## Location Notes
An area of common scrubland on the outskirts of Blackburn. It is popular with dog walkers.

1) Standing in for the usual Class 150, 156429 descends the bank into Blackburn with a Manchester train.
*April, 15:00, 55mm*

## Public Transport
Lancashire United, service 225, operates every 30 minutes between Bolton, Blackburn and Clitheroe and passes the location on Whalley New Road.

## Amenities
There are several pubs and shops near the junction with the ring road. Blackburn town centre is just over a mile away.

## Photographic Notes
The best shot is an early evening view of trains departing Blackburn up the steep bank when they are powering hard towards Clitheroe.

There is a limited view looking north. For both views the grass can start to impact later in the year as it grows higher.

2) heads north out of Blackburn with a Clitheroe service.
*April, 15:00, 90mm*

There has been palisade fencing erected recently though this should not cause too many problems as you can stand higher on the hill.

# Brownhill, Blackburn

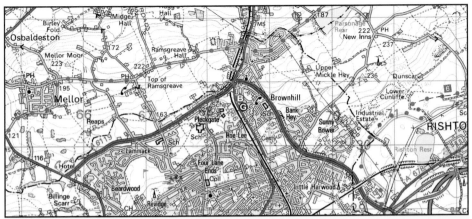

**Postcode: BB1 9AY**     **Lat N53:46:13**     **Long W02:28:48**

## Road Directions

From the M6, Junction 31: Take the A59 east towards Blackburn. After about a mile get into the right hand lane as you will need to turn right onto the A677 through all the traffic lights. After a further 4 miles fork left onto the A6119 ring road and continue for two miles until you see the Knowles Arms pub on the right. Be aware of the speed cameras. Get in the 'Town Centre' lane, on the right, and follow the 'Town Centre' signs onto the A666. It is a strange roundabout/traffic lights junction. Just before the first houses on the right, opposite Ruby Street, you will see the footpath leading through a bridge under the railway.

There is on street parking just after you pass the bridge.

3) 57305 drags 390051 north towards Clitheroe on a diversion over the S&C.
*February, 15:30, 115mm*

# Wilpshire

## Location Notes

Wilpshire Tunnel marks the point the line leaves the urban area of Blackburn and enters the Ribble Valley. There are two locations here, one at each end of the tunnel.

1) #1, Taking the slow route, 66108 heads a southbound departmental working from Carlisle to Crewe Basford Hall. *March, 15:00, 80mm*

## Public Transport

Ramsgreave and Wilpshire station is about a 15 minute walk from the south end of the tunnel (location #2) but around 30 minutes from location, #1, at the north end. Lancashire United, service 225, operates half hourly along the A666 from Bolton and Blackburn.

## Amenities

The are shops on the A666 towards Blackburn.

## Accommodation

There is a Premier inn located on the A59 opposite the BAE Systems Airfield at Salmesbury.

2) #1, 150274 heads north to Clitheroe. *April, 15:00, 40mm*

## Photographic Notes

#1 is at the north end of the tunnel and is a quiet bridge around 500 yards north of the tunnel entrance. The light here is best for afternoon shots of trains heading towards Blackburn. Shots looking towards the tunnel are also possible but the light will usually be wrong. The cuttings, deeper looking south, are tree-lined so shadows can be a problem in winter. A footpath leads north from this bridge to a field giving late afternoon and evening views, again for southbound trains. This is an open field so shadows are not a problem here.

Location #2 is on the B6245 road and is looking down to the southern tunnel portal. Again this is best for afternoon shots but the cutting is very deep and you get little warning of trains approaching. This bridge suffers from traffic noise so will be unsuitable for videos.

3) #1, 150274 heads north to Clitheroe. *April, 15:00, 70mm*

# Wilpshire

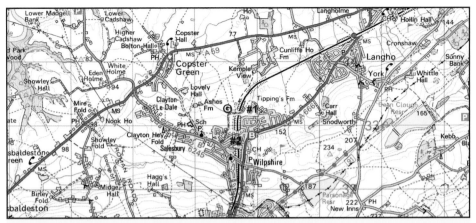

**Postcode: BB1 9HY**　　　　　**Lat N53:47:39**　　　　　**Long W02:28:37**

## Road Directions

From the M6, Junction 31: Take the A59 east towards Clitheroe. Follow this for 6 miles turning right at the traffic lights in Clayton-le-Dale onto the B6245. After about half a mile there is a church on the left and a speed camera. Take the next left into Vicarage Lane. This quickly becomes untarmaced, keep to the left and follow it down the hill and you will eventually reach bridge #1. There is plenty of room to park here. The footpath to the field is on the left before the bridge.

For location #2 continue past Vicarage Lane and you will come to the bridge. Park on the road before it.

4) #2, 60007 emerges from the tunnel and heads south to Blackburn with a loaded test run to and from Carnforth.
*April, 14:15, 135mm*

# Barrow, Lamb Roe

## Location Notes
One of a series of very quiet foot crossings on a straight section of line in the middle of countryside. The footpath leads across fields and can be very muddy in places.

1) 150134 approaches the foot crossing with a northbound Manchester to Clitheroe service.
*January, 10:15, 80mm*

## Public Transport
The road through Barrow is well served by Lancashire United buses with service 225 every 30 minutes between Clitheroe, Blackburn and Bolton, an hourly 280/X80 between Preston and Skipton and half hourly 28/29 from Burnley.

## Amenities
The Spread Eagle pub is a short distance away on the main road. There is a McDonalds and a supermarket/petrol station at the A59 services.

## Photographic Notes
The line runs roughly north to south so the sun will be head on around midday and will favour southbound trains heading towards Blackburn.

2) A southbound 150139 is the train to beware of.
*February, 14:30, 75mm*

There is a line of trees on the east side of the line so shadows could be a problem in a morning but it is far more open on the west side. A new signal has been erected to the north but this should not cause any problems as it will be in the background of the shot.

As you are in the middle of fields there should not be any noise to disturb videographers.

# Barrow, Lamb Roe

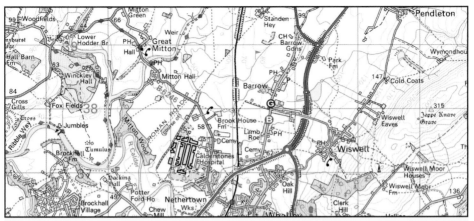

**Postcode: BB7 9BN**              **Lat N53:50:05**              **Long W02:24:39**

## Road Directions

From the M6, Junction 31: Take the A59 east towards Clitheroe for about 9 miles. You will see Whalley viaduct on the right. Go straight over the next two roundabouts (the second leads to the services) and turn left at the third onto the A671 towards Clitheroe. Turn left again after about 300 yards towards Barrow. Pass through the village and after leaving it you will approach a row of houses on the right with the Spread Eagle pub at the far end.

Just before the first house, opposite the entrance to 'Ashleigh', the footpath is signposted over the farm gate. Follow the path across the left side of the first field. It then crosses into the next field, which you need to walk along the right side of, for about ¾ of its length before it crosses back into the original field. The foot crossing is located in the small wood at the end.

3) 60096 makes light work of a Carlisle to Crewe rail train heading south towards Blackburn.
*January, 10:15, 80mm*

# Horrocksford Junction

## Location Notes

A road bridge over the line by the junction where a siding leads into the Castle Cement works and the local units terminating at Clitheroe come to cross over the tracks to return to Manchester.

1) 66113 reaches journey's end at Clitheroe with a train from Mossend and slows before reversing into the cement works.
*March, 12:00, 80mm*

## Public Transport

Clitheroe has an hourly service from Manchester and the location is about a 15 minute walk from the bus and railway stations.

### Amenities

There is a wide range of shops and pubs in Clitheroe town centre.

### Photographic Notes

The bridge is reasonably busy. The southern side is a separate footpath bridge, and there is no path on the northern side. However, it is safe to take shots from either corner of the northern side.

The light is usually best for southbound trains with the sun being head on around 15:00.

Early in the morning the sun will be on the front of northbound trains. Traffic noise will be a problem for videographers.

2) 57307 drags 390052 past a northbound 222014.
*May, 09:45, 280mm*

# Horrocksford Junction

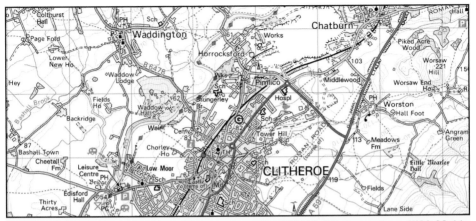

**Postcode: BB7 2BG**      **Lat N53:52:48**      **Long W02:23:11**

## Road Directions

From the M6, Junction 31: Follow the A59 east for approximately 14 miles. You will pass two turnings for Clitheroe itself, follow signs for Clitheroe (N) Industrial Estates. Turn left into the A671, Pimlico Link Road. Go straight on at the next roundabout heading towards the cement works and turn left towards Clitheroe on Pimllico Road just as you are approaching a level crossing. Park before you reach the signs for the weak bridge. From the east on the A59 the Pimlico Link Road is signposted as the A671 to Clitheroe.

3) 150223 is about to shunt over the crossing by the cement works before heading back to Bolton.
*May, 09:15, 225mm*

# Rimington

## Location Notes

This location is a quiet farm bridge in open countryside.

1) 66174 with empty tanks from Mossend to the Castle Cement plant at Horrocksford.
   *May, 11:30, 115mm*

## Public Transport

There are no useful public transport links to this location.

## Amenities

The nearest are local shops and pubs in Chatburn. The closest supermarkets are in Clitheroe about 5 miles away.

## Photographic Notes

There are shots available in both directions here and you will receive plenty of warning of approaching trains as the line is staright for a good distance in both directions. The sun will be side on around late morning so afternoons will favour trains heading east towards Hellifield.

The location is in the middle of fields so there should not be much in the way of noise affecting videos.

2) drags 390020 south through Rimington, Preston-bound.
   *May, 11:00, 135mm*

# Rimington

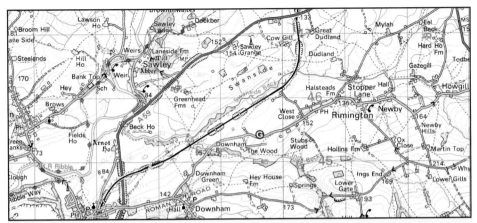

**Postcode: BB7 4DR**     **Lat N53:54:27**     **Long W02:16:60**

## Road Directions

From M6, Junction 31: Follow the A59 east for around 14 miles passing Clitheroe. You will see the A671, Pimlico Link Road on the left, signposted Clitheroe Industrial Estates. About ½ mile after this turn left towards Chatburn. At the end of this road turn right into the village. The road to Rimington is signposted on the right just after you pass the Brown Cow pub in the village. Cross the A59 and after about ½ mile turn left into Green Lane. Follow this lane for about a mile. You will pass an entrance on the right to Wood Farm and immediately on the left is the entrance to a property called Denisfield. The footpath leads through this property - it used to be a house but it has been demolished, though there was some activity at the time of our last visit so it may be being rebuilt. The official path goes to the right once through the gate, skirting the pond and round to the back of the property. Make your way to corner of field and climb through into next field which leads to the bridge.

3) 57303 and 390017 heading north with another S&C diversion.
*May, 11:45, 135mm*

# Hellifield Green

## Location Notes

A field between a main road and the railway. It is a fairly exposed location.

1) 221112 rounds the curve after coming off the S&C with a diverted Glasgow-Preston service.
*February, 14:30, 135mm*

## Public Transport

Pennine Bus, service 580, runs hourly (2 hourly Saturdays) between Skipton and Settle along the A65 and the nearest stop in Hellifield is about ½ mile away. Hellifield station is about 1 mile away.

## Amenities

There are several local shops in Hellifield Village about ½ mile away.

## Photographic Notes

This is primarily an afternoon shot of trains leaving Hellifield heading towards Blackburn. The distant signal adds to the shot, though note it does not work. Line speed is low here and trains are climbing but the nearby road carries quite a few lorries so this may impact on video sound recordings.

2) 66102 slows with an eastbound working from the Clitheroe works.
*April, 18:00, 45mm*

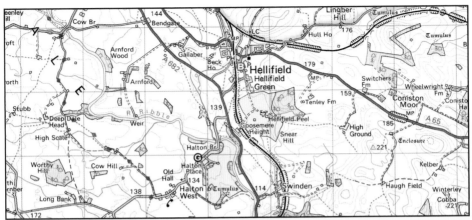

**Postcode: BD23 4LJ**          **Lat N53:59:48**          **Long W02:13:24**

## Road Directions

From the Lancashire area either leave the M6 at Junction 31 and take the A59 east towards Skipton as far as Gisburn or from the M65, Junction 13: Take the A682 towards Kendal. (Note: junction 12 is also signposted for the A682 but this will not take you the right way). At Gisburn turn right onto the A59 for about 200 yards before turning left to continue on the A682 towards Settle. After about 5 miles watch out for a left hand turn signposted to Halton West. Turn into here to park - the footpath into the field starts opposite the entrance to this road.

From the west on the A65, turn right onto the A682 towards Nelson after passing through Long Preston and the road to Halton West is on the right about 300yds after you pass a 'Low Bridge 3 miles' sign. There is a left hand turn in Hellifield village signposted 'Nelson' if you are coming from the east. This road brings you out by the low bridge sign where you should turn left onto the A682.

3) 66102 slows with an eastbound working from the Clitheroe works.
*Photo by Neil Harvey, March, 15:30, 75mm*

# Little North Western

## General Notes

The route from Skipton to Morecambe and Heysham was known as the 'Little North Western' to differentiate it from the London and North Western Railways West Coast Main Line. Trains today take a slightly longer route, via Carnforth, following the closure of the section from Wennington, along the River Lune, through Lancaster Green Ayre. Most of this line is still in use as a footpath/cycle track and the bridge over the river now forms part of the town's ring road.

The line is double track apart from the section between Morecambe and Heysham. Between Skipton and Settle Junction the route now forms part of the much more important Midland Route to Carlisle. From Settle junction to Carnforth there are now no intermediate signal boxes following the demolition of the box at Wennington. Trains run on the West Coast Main Line for a short distance before turning off at Hest Bank to reach Morecambe. Trains have to reverse at Morecambe to gain access to the single track line to Heysham Port.

1) 156470 and 498 head east from Carlisle to Leeds.
*April, 11:15, 80mm*

## Passenger Traffic

The main service along this route is an infrequent, 4 or 5 daily trains, operated by Northern's Pacer or Sprinter units. These are supplemented at the eastern end between Skipton and Settle by Carlise bound trains formed of 156 or 158 units, and at the western end a shuttle service operates between Lancaster and Morecabe, generally using 156s. One train per day continues to Heysham Port to connect with the Isle of Man ferry.

2) 66414 and 417 with the Heysham flask.
*November, 15:45, 75mm*

## Freight Traffic

There is no regular freight traffic over the central section of the line. East of Settle Junction through freights from Carlise, mainly coal and departmental workings can be seen (Note: Some of these will rejoin the Blackburn line at Hellifleld).

There is a weekly Nuclear Flask train to the power station at Heysham.

## Occasional Traffic

The main source of interesting workings over the section east of Carnforth is the West Coast Railway Company which has its base there. There are regularly Empty Coaching Stock moves along the line in order to position stock for railtours. The line,

3) 66560 heads south with an engineers train.
*June, 13:30, 65mm*

being quiet with passenger trains, is the preferred choice for them to test run locomotives, both steam and diesel. East of Settle Junction more workings can be seen as trains come off the Settle to Carlisle line.

# Little North Western

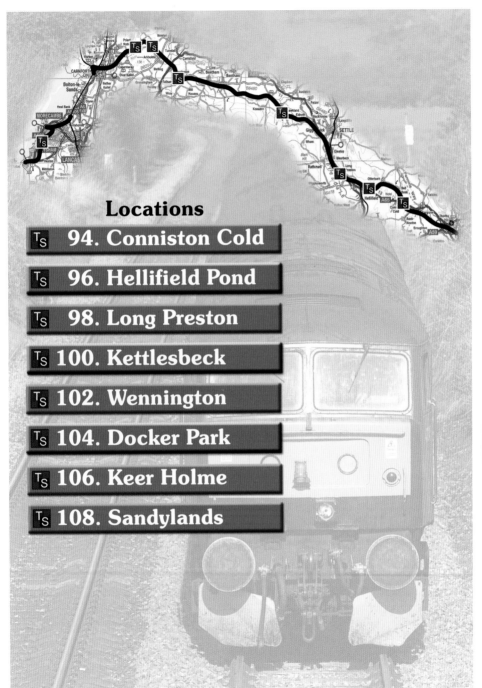

## Locations

TS **94. Conniston Cold**

TS **96. Hellifield Pond**

TS **98. Long Preston**

TS **100. Kettlesbeck**

TS **102. Wennington**

TS **104. Docker Park**

TS **106. Keer Holme**

TS **108. Sandylands**

# Conniston Cold

## Location notes

This location is two private fields situated on either side of the line on the side of the Aire Valley.
These are wide, open fields and so will be exposed. The fields on the west of the line look out across the river valley.

1) 66525 catches the last of the evening light as it heads a coal working to Ratcliffe power station.
*April, 19:00, 80mm*

## Public transport

Gargrave station is about 1½ miles away and is served by trains from Leeds.

Pennine, service 580, operates every hour (2 hourly on Saturdays) along the A65 between Skipton, Hellifield and Settle. The nearest stops are ¼ mile away in Coniston Cold village.

## Amenities

There is the Anchor Inn, a 'Brewers Fayre' pub ½ mile to the east on the A65. Gargrave has several pubs, a convenience store and a chip shop.

## Accommodation

The Coniston Hotel is on the A65 just west of Coniston Cold if you have plenty of money. Otherwise there are guest houses in Gargrave.

## Photographic notes

There is an early morning shot from the field on the eastern side of the line for northbound trains - a public footpath runs through the bottom half of this. The sun will be off the front quite soon though, so it will be back lit for much of the day.

In the afternoon and evening you need to be in the field on the west side of the line, there being a metal gate just on the other side of the bridge. The sun will be side on around 17:00 so will favour southbound trains before that and northbound trains later in the evening.
Depending on the direction of the wind, traffic on the A65 may impact on video recordings.

2) 158860 heads south with a Leeds service.
*April, 16:45, 40mm*

3) 158860 heads north to Carlisle.
*April, 19:00, 80mm*

# Conniston Cold

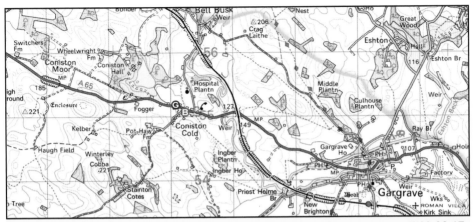

**Postcode: BD23 4EF**        **Lat N53:59:28**        **Long W02:08:17**

## Road directions

The location is situated on the main A65 trunk road which runs from Skipton to Kendal.

If coming from the west you will pass through Coniston Cold, cross a narrow river bridge, then see the railway over bridge.

From the east, leave Gargrave village, passing a canal lock on your left just before the Anchor Inn and continue until you see the radio mast on your left.

There is a small lay-by, on the eastbound side, immediately after the bridge where you can park.

4) 47760 passes over the A65 bridge with 'The Hadrian' charter from Stevenage to Carlisle.
*Photo by Neil Harvey, Month, 10:00, 110mm*

# Hellifield Pond

## Location notes

This location is situated on the western side of the Pennines, on a small, but busy for the area, road heading out of Hellifield. The weather may change at any time and it would be advisable to have warm clothing to hand, although you are never far from your car should the weather change.

1) 66059 heads Anglo-Scottish coal south towards the Yorkshire power stations.
*Photo by Richard Tearle, September, 12:30, 60mm*

## Public transport

Hellifield station is about a mile away. There is a train roughly every 2 hours in each direction to Leeds and Carlisle. There are also 4 trains a day from Lancaster and Morecambe. From the station it would be a good 20 minutes walk.
Pennine Bus, service 580, runs hourly (2 hourly Saturdays) between Skipton and Settle along the A65. The nearest stop is in Hellifield about a mile away.

## Amenities

There are no amenities at the location but Hellifield boasts a number of shops and pubs. There is also a cafe at the station.

## Photographic notes

There are two eastbound shots at this location and one westbound. By following the road back towards Hellifield it is possible to get a shot of the trains passing a small pond and trees, hence the name for this location. There are also east and westbound shots from on top of the bridge itself. The eastbound shot is best in the morning, and on a cloudy day the westbound is good then. In the afternoon the 'wrong side' shot is still favoured for

2) 60028 with a Drax to Newbiggin gypsum working.
*Photo by Richard Tearle, September, 13:00, 50mm*

the westbound shot. From the pond shooting spot it is just possible to see the semaphore signal protecting the crossing which will give you enough notice that a northbound train is approaching. It is also possible to see the westbound trains in the distance for a mad dash back to the bridge.

# Hellifield Pond

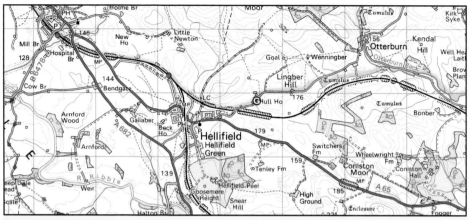

**Postcode: BD23 4JP**     **Lat N54:00:23**     **Long W02:12:41**

## Road directions

Coming north on the A65 turn off to the right just south of Hellifield on the road signposted Otterburn. If you reach the middle of Hellifield you have gone too far.

Following the road until it goes over the railway, from the Hellifield direction, you will see a field entrance that has space for a couple of cars without blocking access to the field. There is also one space on the other side of the road on the Hellifield side of the bridge. Other parking may be found further along the road towards Otterburn.

3) 70003 pilots 66154 past the pond with a Swindon to Leeds charter.
*Photo by David Dawson, April, 10:45, 80mm*

# Long Preston

## Location Notes

A view across a field to the line from a busy main road on the edge of Long Preston village.

1) 66174 pilots 66037 on a rare Saturday departmental working from Carlisle to Warrington.
*February, 15:30, 45mm*

## Public Transport

Long Preston station is just under ½ mile away.

There is an hourly service along the main road operated by Pennine Buses (service 580) between Skipton and Settle (no service Sundays and only 2 hourly Saturdays)

## Amenities

There are a couple of pubs and shops in Long Preston Village.

## Photographic Notes

The line runs North-West to South-East at this point so the light here is really only best for early morning southbound trains, but of course if it is cloudy then it could be useable most of the day. The main advantage of this location is that if time is limited it is a handy location because it is situated on the main A65 with parking next to where you stand.

Heavy traffic means this location is not suitable for videos.

2) 144001 heads south past two cameramen who've found their way here without Trainspots.
*Photo by Chris Nevard, May, 11:30, 40mm*

# Long Preston

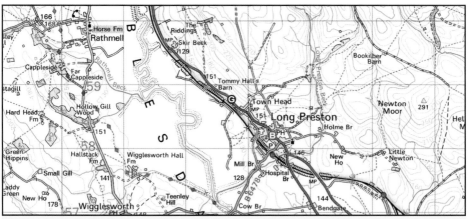

**Postcode: BD23 4QL**     **Lat N54:01:23**     **Long W02:15:50**

## Road Directions

This location is on the A65 with room for two cars to park at the top of the small lane.

From the east after passing through Long Preston village the location is on the left immediately after the national speed limit sign, from the Settle direction as you approach Long Preston look out for a speed camera sign on the right and the lane is between this and the '30mph Long Preston' signs.

3) 20213 and 37038 head south towards Hellifield with a private charter for Direct Rail Services.
*August, 11:15, 100mm*

# Kettlesbeck

## Location Notes

A quiet road bridge over the line in countryside. The road leads only to farms so traffic is very light.

1) 144007 ambles along with a service from Leeds.
   *August, 11:30, 80mm*

## Public Transport

Clapham Station is to the north, about 2 miles away, along country lanes. There is no bus service.

## Amenities

There are none in the area. There are several snack bars along the A65 and there is a pub in Austwick.

## Photographic Notes

The line here is on a curve. The bridge offers good views in both directions, however the field on the east side is better for westbound trains. The sun will be head on for eastbound trains around 10:00 so the ideal shot is from 11:00 to early afternoon for trains heading towards Hellifield.
In late afternoon the sun will come round enough for westbound workings.
For videos, traffic noise will not be a problem; if anything can be heard on audio recordings it will be the wind or the sheep.

2) A livery jumble from 153330 and 144007 as they head west.
   *March, 15:00, 80mm*

# Kettlesbeck

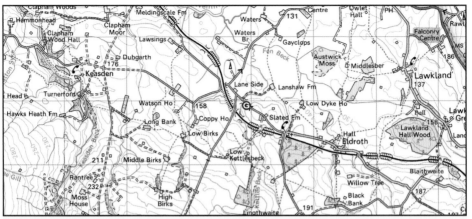

**Postcode: LA2 8AF**                    **Lat N54:05:16**                    **Long W02:23:16**

## Road Directions

From the M6, Junction 36: Take the A65 east towards Skipton. You pass through the outskirts of Ingleton and Clapham. After the B6480 joins from the right near Clapham you then pass a turning on the right signposted Keasden. A mile further on is a left turn to Austwick, take the turning on the right after that (Orcaber Lane) towards Eldroth.

After about a mile you will see the railway in front of you. Turn left into Eldroth Road before the railway and first right towards the bridge, signposted High Birks.

If travelling from the east along the A65 the turning towards Eldroth is on the left just under ½ mile after you pass the roads to Austwick (on the right) and Lawkland (on the left).

3) 33207 top & tails with 47826 on a private charter from Carnforth to Carnforth via Blackburn.
*January, 12:45 135mm*

# Wennington

## Location Notes

Wennington is a small, quiet village. The road running through it is fairly quiet and you are unlikely to come across many people.

1) 47851 heads east past the, now removed, remains of the signal box. Viewed from the second location near the station.
   *April, 10:15, 65mm*

## Public Transport

Wennington station is served by 4 or 5 trains a day running between Lancaster and Leeds. Stagecoach, services 80 and 81B, both run approximately every 2 hours from Lancaster Bus Station to Wennington.

## Amenities

There is little in the immediate area. The Bridge Inn pub is less than ½ mile south along the B6480.

## Accommodation

There is a Holiday Inn and also a Premier Inn located just west of junction 34 of the M6.

2) 47826 heads west to Carnforth with a coach in need of restoration.
   *February, 14:15, 55mm*

## Photographic Notes

There are several viewpoints in the area.

The best one is a morning shot taken looking west from beside a farm gate on the B6480 as an eastbound train approaches Wennington. From the farm gate a footpath runs down to the line and there is a foot crossing with a stile which enables a tight angle in the afternoon for westbound workings. These can also be photographed from the station. There is an additional morning shot from the bridge nearer the station.

# Wennington

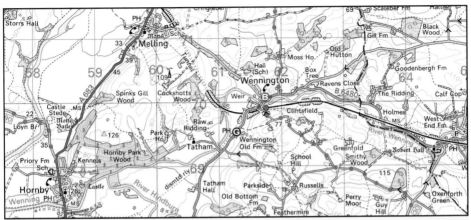

**Postcode: LA2 8NL**        **Lat N54:07:22**        **Long W02:35:30**

## Road Directions

From the M6, Junction 34: Take the A683 east towards Kirkby Lonsdale. You pass through Caton and about 3 miles afterwards you need to turn right onto the B6480 towards Bentham. Pass through Wray and you will see an old railway track bed on the left. After you pass the Bridge Inn there is a farm gate on the left (with room for one car to park in front) immediately before the 'Wennington' and 30mph signs. From this farm gate is the morning view west. You will see the foot crossing from here too. Continue over the two railway bridges (one the disused line and one the operational one) and on the right is Wennington station where there is ample parking. If coming from the east take the B6480 signposted Bentham, from the A65 near Clapham. Pass through Bentham to Wennington and the station is just after the river bridge.

3) 70003 and 66164 heading east around the curve towards the station with a Pathfinder tour to Leeds.
   *April, 10:15, 55mm*

# Docker Park

## Location Notes

An over bridge carrying a quiet lane over the railway in a rural area. There are few cars using the bridge and no pedestrians. The railway is in a slight cutting to the east with a pleasing rural view to the west.

1) 37069 and 607 take a Mossend to Derby via Carnforth and Hellifield test train south. Viewed from the 2nd bridge.
*Photo by Anthony Roberts, May, 15:00, 35mm*

## Public Transport

Stagecoach, service 81A, operates every 2 hours from Lancaster to Arkholme, Bay Horse, from where it would be about a 25-30 minutes walk.

## Amenities

There are none near the location: the Bay Horse in Arkholme is the nearest pub, the nearest shops are in Kirkby Lonsdale 4-5 miles away.

## Photographic Notes

There are shots in both directions from the bridge. The best is looking west for trains heading towards Settle Junction from late morning until early afternoon. After that the light will favour westbound trains, though the shallow cutting is prominent in this direction. Traffic is very light so unlikely to disturb videos.

There is also a second bridge in farmland just to the south of the main road bridge.

2) 47245 heads a Whitby charter south towards Leeds.
*Photo by Anthony Roberts, April, 15:30, 180mm*

# Docker Park

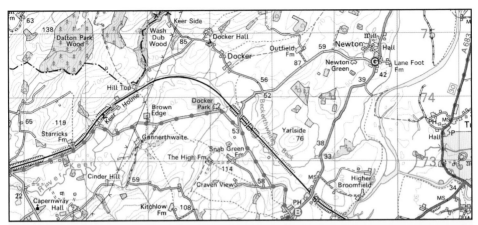

**Postcode: LA6 2PA**          **Lat N54:09:26**          **Long W02:39:09**

## Road Directions

From the M6, Junction 35: Take the short spur of the A601(M) towards Over Kellet. Turn left at the end onto the B6254 towards Kirkby Lonsdale. Follow this road for about 5 miles through Over Kellet until you reach Arkholme. Turn left at the Bay Horse pub and follow this lane for a mile towards Docker until you reach the bridge.

There is room to park on the bridge.

3) 144008 heads for the seaside at Morecambe with a local Northern service from Leeds.
*March, 10:45, 135mm*

# Keer Holme

## Location Notes

In the middle of pleasant countryside, this location is a quiet road bridge spanning the railway.

1) 144013 heads for Leeds with a Northern working from Morecambe.
*April, 10:15, 50mm*

## Public Transport

There is no public transport to this location

## Amenities

The nearest are in and around Carnforth about 5 miles away which has supermarkets, local shops and pubs. There is a truck stop near the A601(M).

## Photographic Notes

The light is best for eastbound trains until around 10:00. From then until early afternoon the sun will favour shots taken of westbound trains from the southern side of the bridge. If the hedge has not been cut recently a step ladder may be of use for this. During late afternoon and early

2) 150273 provides a break from 144s on the Morcambe service.
*February, 10:00, 55mm*

evening, trains heading towards Carnforth will have sun on the front, depending on the time of the year, from the northern side of the bridge.

The location is close to a few farms but little else so there is little to disturb audio sound tracks.

# Keer Holme

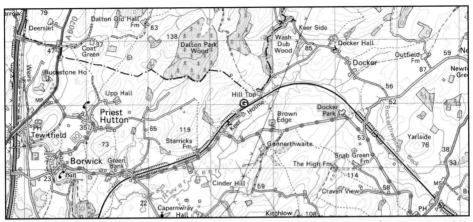

**Postcode: LA6 1AW**                **Lat N54:09:31**                **Long W02:41:02**

## Road Directions

From the M6, Junction 35: Take the short spur of the A601(M) east towards Over Kellet. Turn left at the end onto the B6254. After about ½ mile you will pass through a single track section of road, turn left at Over Kellet village green towards Capernwray. Follow this road for about 2 miles and turn left at the end by the church. Take the next road on the right, signposted Keer Holme. After about ½ mile following the railway on the left the road bends to the right towards Arkholme. Take the lane on the left here, Keer Holme Lane, and this leads to the bridge.

There is room for one car by the farm gate just over the bidge, otherwise there is plenty of room on the verge when the lane straightens out afterwards.

3) Catching the setting sun, 47786 and 47851 top & tail a WCRC empty stock move from Norwich to Carnforth.
*October, 17:45, 120mm*

# Sandylands, Fanny House Farm

## Location Notes

A road bridge, carrying a busy secondary road, over the Heysham Branch.

1) DRS enters the Branch Line Clagging Cup with contestants 37029 and 37229 heading to Heysham.
*Photo by Richard Stiles, August, 15:00, 120mm*

## Public Transport

Stagecoach, service 2, operates every 20 minutes from Lancaster and Morecambe to Kingsway in Heysham near the bridge.

## Amenities

There is a Tesco Metro on the A589 in Heysham. Morecambe is two miles away with various shops and pubs; there is also a large ASDA just off the main road from Lancaster, turn left at the first roundabout after passing under the Main Line.

## Accommodation

There is a Holiday Inn and also a Premier Inn located just west of junction 34 of the M6.

## Photographic Notes

The best shot is an afternoon view of trains heading into Heysham. The sun is head on around midday. There is a shot looking towards Heysham too but as this is facing south it will be into the light.

2) 144007 heads to Morecambe, where it will reverse and head back to Leeds.
*February, 13:30, 55mm*

The road is quite busy and there are no pavements, however there is just enough room to stand on verges safely. Traffic on the bridge means it is not really suitable for video recordings, the lack of footpaths also means tripods are not recommended.

# Sandylands, Fanny House Farm

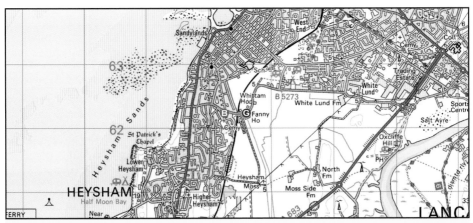

**Postcode: LA3 3EF**　　　　　**Lat N54:03:10**　　　　　**Long W02:52:50**

## Road Directions

From the M6, Junction 34: Take the A683 towards Lancaster. When you reach the one-way system keep to the right, following the A683 towards Morecambe. As you cross the river move to the left to stay on the A683. You will pass under the West Coast Main Line. At the second roundabout turn left towards Heysham. Go through the next set of lights and turn right at next roundabout onto the A5273, Oxcliffe Road. Go straight on at the roundabout past Matalan and follow the road until you reach the bridge. There is room for on street parking after the bridge.

3) 37602 and 20305 unusually outnumbered by wagons on a trip down to the plant at Heysham.
May, 15:00, 85mm

# WCML - Carnforth to Carlisle

## General Notes

This is one of the most scenic sections of the route from London to Glasgow, passing through the Lake District with the rolling mountains providing the backdrop. Electrified throughout, it is mainly two track with passing loops.

There is the long climb, in both directions, to Shap with the summit located between Thrimby and Greenholme.

## Passenger Traffic

Virgin operates two trains an hour, in each direction, throughout the route. One being a Pendolino from London and the other a Voyager from Birmingham.

Trans Pennine Express run a roughly hourly Manchester to Scotland service using their 185 units either singly or in pairs.

## Freight Traffic

Intermodal Anglo-Scottish trains are the staple traffic throughout the length of the route operated by DB Schenker with 92s, Freightliner with 86s and DRS with 66s.

In addition there is coal traffic from DB Schenker and Freightliner as well as infrastructure trains from both operators.

Royal Mail class 325s operate several times a day, these workings can also be operated by loco hauling the units.

The log train to Chirk operated by Colas 66s has been running this way each afternoon, however it has started occasionally being routed via the Settle and Carlisle line instead.

## Occasional Traffic

The route is popular with special excursions heading for Carlisle or Scotland.

West Coast Railway Company has its base at Carnforth so is a source of regular Empty Coaching Stock trains to other parts of the country to form rail tours.

The Network Rail New Measurement HST has a weekly diagram along the route.

Light engine movements by DRS are common as are Virgin's class 57 being moved light engine back to Longsight for maintenance.

1) 390019 heads south with a Euston-bound working.
*November 09:15, 145mm*

2) 92039 heads south at Docker with the logs to Chirk.
*March, 12:30, 120mm*

3) 57301 heads south to Longsight for maintenance.
*November, 10:45, 40mm*

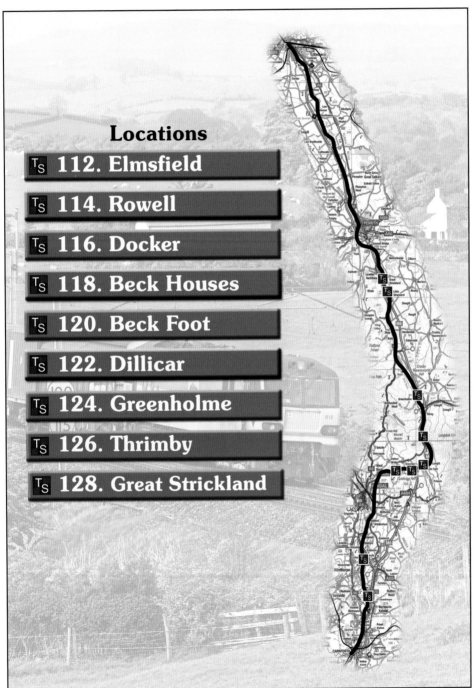

## Locations

TS **112. Elmsfield**

TS **114. Rowell**

TS **116. Docker**

TS **118. Beck Houses**

TS **120. Beck Foot**

TS **122. Dillicar**

TS **124. Greenholme**

TS **126. Thrimby**

TS **128. Great Strickland**

# Elmsfield

## Location Notes

This location is a bridge carrying a quiet lane over the railway. There are views in both directions.

1) Reflections from the days when mail trains existed. 90028 heads north to Scotland with the Christmas post.
*December, 14:45, 55mm*

## Public Transport

Stagecoach, service 555, links Lancaster and Kendal hourly and passes the end of the road, though the nearest bus stop is in Holme Village about 15 minutes walk away.

## Amenities

There are none near the location.

## Photographic Notes

The best shots here are in the afternoon, lunch time to late afternoon for southbound trains and after that for northbound. Whilst the overhead wires can pose a slight problem from bridge height it is possible to climb carefully lower on either side. The area to the south of the bridge can be flooded after heavy rain which can add to the shot in that direction. Metal refuges have been built on the embankment recently which alters the northbound shot slightly. There is only occasional traffic on the lane to disturb video sound.

2) 66147 heads a coal working south.
*May, 16:30, 75mm*

3) 390041 heads south to London.
*April, 18:45, 130mm*

# Elmsfield

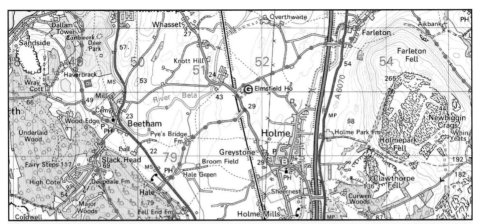

**Postcode: LA6 1RJ**  **Lat N54:12:36**  **Long W02:44:34**

## Road Directions

From The M6, Junction 35: Take the A601(M) towards Carnforth. At the end turn right onto the A6 towards Milnthorpe and at the next roundabout fork right onto the A6070 towards Burton in Kendal. Just about a mile after passing through Burton turn left onto the B6384, signposted Holme and Milnthorpe.

After passing through Holme village you will see the railway on the left. There is a green footbridge over the field then you will see a road bridge over the railway. Turn left to this bridge.

There is room for two cars to park on the verge just after you cross it.

4) 67005 returns the empty Royal Train to its base at Wolverton.
*May, 15:30, 220mm*

# Rowell

## Location Notes
This is a quiet location in the southern Lakeland fells. There are a couple of houses and a dog kennels in the vicinity of the railway bridge.

1) 92012 winds its way south through the rolling Lake District hills with an Enterprise working to Eastleigh.
*Photo by Chris Nevard, May, 17:15, 180mm*

## Public Transport
Stagecoach, service 555, operates hourly between Lancaster and Kendal.
The nearest stop is in Ackenthwaite on the B6385 from where it would be about a 20-25 minute walk.

## Amenities
None at the location, the nearest being in Milnthorpe which is about 3 miles away.

## Accommodation
The Crooklands Hotel is located near to the M6.

## Photographic Notes
The morning shot is from the bottom corner of a field and is slightly limited due to the hedge and the new barn in the farm below. The afternoon shot is altogether different as there are various angles to be had from the lane to the west of the bridge.

2) 86632 and 639 provide the horsepower for a Basford Hall-bound intermodal.
*July, 17:30, 115mm*

A step ladder might be useful for some people due to the height of the hedge; the lane is narrow but very quiet.
An additional high level view is available in the field through the gate on the left after you cross the bridge.
Videoing will probably only be disturbed by the occasional passing car going to the kennels or by the geese and dogs nearby.

# Rowell

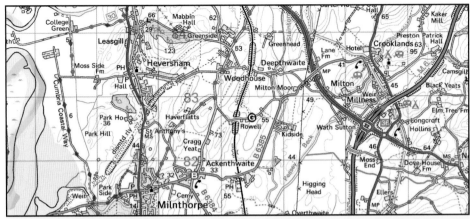

**Postcode: LA7 7LU**          **Lat N54:14:14**          **Long W02:44:59**

## Road Directions

From the M6, Junction 36: Turn briefly east onto the A65 towards Skipton, turning left at the next roundabout, again onto the A65, towards Crooklands and Kendal. You will pass under the M6 and just before the Crooklands Hotel turn left onto the B6385, signposted Milnthorpe.

Follow this road for about a mile. After a turning signposted Heaversham you pass a large farm and the road bends to the right.

You will see a stone wall on the right, which is actually a river bridge, and the wide turning on the right immediately after this, signposted Rowell, is the start of Rowell Lane. There is nowhere on the lane to park so you can either park here (about a 10 minute walk up lane to the location) or continue up the lane, over the railway, and to the top where there is a fairly wide road on which you can park (5 minutes walk).

The morning location is accessed through the field on the east side of the bridge with the transmitter aerial. There is a gap in the hedge in the bottom corner behind this.

3) 66428 heads south with a Malcolm intermodal bound for the Daventry International Railfreight Terminal.
*November, 10:30, 80mm*

# Docker

## Location Notes

This is a bridge on a fairly quiet lane giving views in either direction.

It is a fairly exposed location, although parking is close by so you can shelter in your vehicle if necessary.

1) 66411 *Eddie the Engine* provides minimal $CO_2$ while moving the Tesco Express uphill enroute to Grangemouth.
   *April, 09:45, 115mm*

## Public Transport

Service 106/107 operates about every 2 hours from Kendal to Penrith and passes the end of the lane on the A685, however there are no official stops in the vicinity.

## Amenities

The nearest is Morrisons on the outskirts of Kendal about 3 miles away.

## Photographic Notes

The preferred shot is for southbound trains from just after lunch to late afternoon. Since one of the wires on the overheads was raised, the westward shot of northbound trains is much better now, and the sun will be on the front until lunch time. The lane is fairly quiet so traffic noise shouldn't affect video recording too much.

2) 220015 speeds south with a Birmingham to Glasgow service.
   *March, 14:00, 160mm*

# Docker

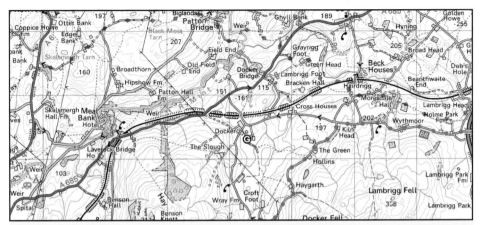

**Postcode: LA8 0DB**       **Lat N54:21:17**       **Long W02:40:32**

## Road Directions

From the M6, Junction 37: Take the A684 west towards Kendal.

You will pass a windfarm on the right. The road drops into a valley, past Hutton Park on the right (with a stone ram statue), then as the road climbs again you will see a sign for a crossroads. Turn right into this lane which is signposted Docker.

Follow this for about ½ mile until you come to a left hand turning signposted to Docker and Grayrigg. Keep on this narrow lane as it drops down until you come to a junction with a postbox: you will see the railway in front of you.

Turn left here and this will bring you to the bridge. There is room for one or two cars to park just before the bridge.

3) 66561 takes a set of auto ballasters south from Shap Quarry to Crewe for overnight WCML possessions.
*April, 13:15, 135mm*

# Beck Houses

## Location Notes

A footpath across a field next to the line. The field spans a dip in the landscape giving viewpoints from either side.

It can be very cold depending on wind direction and there is little shelter.

1) 57012 stands in on the loaded Chirk logs while Colas get their traction sorted.
*September, 15:00, 80mm*

## Public Transport

Services 106/107, operate approximately every 2 hours between Kendal and Penrith and stop in Grayrigg village from where it would be about a 25 minute walk to the location. Alight by the church in the village, walk north for 100 yards and turn right into the lane signposted Lambrigg.

This will lead you eventually to the bridge.

## Amenities

There are no amenities in the area, the nearest is in Kendal about 5 miles away.

## Photographic Notes

As the line runs roughly east to west at this point it is one of the few good places to take daytime pictures of northbound trains. The sun will be on the front for these until around lunch time.

The eastern side of the dip in the field is best for morning northbound shots, the western side for afternoon southbound. Tree clearance has opened up a limited southbound shot from the east side of the field.

2) 66623 hurries an empty spoil train south to Mountsorrel.
*Photo by Tony Callaghan, May, 10:45, 100mm*

# Beck Houses

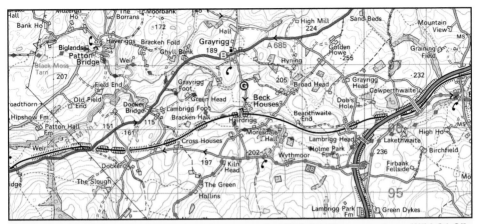

**Postcode: LA8 9ET**        **Lat N02:38:52**        **Long W54:21:35**

## Road Directions

From the M6, Junction 37: Turn onto the A684 towards Sedbergh. After about 300 yards turn sharp left onto a road signposted towards Lambrigg. Follow this road parallel to the M6 for about a mile past a lane going under the M6 then take the next road on the left over the motorway, signposted Docker. After crossing the M6 the lane narrows. Keep going for about ½ mile until you come to the brow of a hill with a bench tucked away on the left on the banking. Turn right down the lane opposite this bench and you will reach an X shaped cross roads, take the left hand fork and this will lead you to a bridge over the railway with a small parking area next to it.

On the right, before the bridge, (opposite the parking area on the east side of the road) is a stile. This will take you into a field. Once you reach the top of the hill you will see the location below.

3) 87002 re-creates West Coast days gone by with the 'Electric Scot Tribute' from Birmingham to Glasgow.
*Photo by Murray Lewis, October, 11:15, 50mm*

# Beck Foot

## Location Notes

This location is a wide grassy area on a quiet lane near the railway and the M6.

1) 66416 speeds around the bend with the Tesco Express to Grangemouth.
   *May, 11:00, 75mm*

## Public Transport

Services 106/107, operate approximately every 2 hours between Kendal and Penrith and stop in Grayrigg village from where it would be about a 45 minute walk to the location.

## Amenities

None in the area. Tebay services near junction 38 of the M6 are the nearest.

## Photographic Notes

Photographs can be taken in both directions here. A few years ago pallisade fencing was erected which spoilt the view somewhat but as the road is slightly higher than the railway its is not a major problem. The fence is also painted green, which makes it less prominent in the shot.

2) 221105 tilts on the curve as it heads north.
   *March, 09:45, 50mm*

The line curves from north/south to east/west in orientation so southbound trains will have the sun on the front until early afternoon. Depending on which point of the curve you stand, northbound trains can still be photographed with sun on the nose until late morning.

# Beck Foot

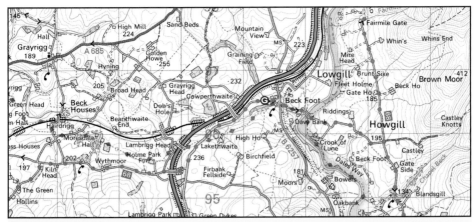

**Postcode: LA8 0BL**                **Lat N54:21:41**                **Long W02:36:10**

## Road Directions

From the M6, Junction 37: Turn east onto the A684 towards Sedbergh for about 300yds before turning sharp left onto a road signposted Lambrigg.

Follow this road alongside the M6 for about 3 miles until it drops down next to the railway. There is plenty of room to park on the verge of the road.

3) 47237 moving support coaches from the DRS base at Carlisle Kingmoor to Crewe.
*March, 09:45, 70mm*

# Dillicar

## Location Notes

This is the classic location in the middle of the Lune Gorge.

There are no roads or footpaths to this location and it involves wading through a river tunnel so it is essential that correct clothes and footwear are worn. As can be expected, once at the location there is little in the way of shelter.

1) 92037 takes the late-running Silver Bullet north through the Lune Gorge.
*Photo by Neil Gibson, May, 16:45, 75mm*

## Public Transport

Services 106/107, operate about every 2 hours between Kendal and Penrith and pass the parking point, although there are no official bus stops nearby.

## Amenities

The nearest shops are in Tebay at the services next to the motorway junction.

## Photographic Notes

From the southern end of this location southbound trains will have the sun on their nose from around lunch time until mid-afternoon.

There is no northbound view from this point.

From the northern end, nearer where you emerge from the river, there are views both ways with the best shot being for northbound trains from mid-afternoon, though the main problem will be from shadows from the hills as the sun gets lower.

2) 66193 heads south with a departmental working.
*July, 14:15, 55mm*

You are next to the M6 so the location is not really suitable for audio recording.

# Dillicar

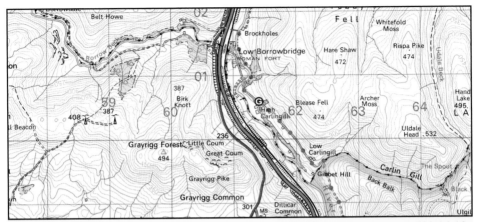

**Postcode: CA10 3XX**              **Lat N54:23:60**              **Long W02:36:10**

## Road Directions

From the M6, Junction 38: Turn south at the roundabout onto the A685 towards Kendal.

You will pass through Tebay village and cross both the railway and motorway and then the road drops down and crosses a small river, with a turning on the left towards Carlingill. The road climbs back up and there is a large parking/viewing area on the left. Park here and continue south on foot.

After about 50 yards you will see a metal gate into a field on the left. Climb this and cut across the field into the bottom corner. Here you will find a small gulley leading into a stream that passes under the motorway. Climb down this and walk *VERY* carefully through the concrete tunnel. The tunnel under the motorway, although of ample height to stand in, is extremely slippery, especially at the bottom end as it emerges into daylight. On the right after the tunnel is a concrete retaining wall on the right. Climb this.

For northbound shots you need to head to the left towards the railway, taking care as there is a concealed ditch that runs through the area. For southbound shots you have to climb up towards the motorway and walk south for some distance next to the crash barrier.

3) Checking the West Coast Main Line for defects and irregularities, 43089 provides electric power to the NMT.
*April, 12:30, 75mm*

# Greenholme

## Location Notes

A quiet lane spanning both the M6 and the railway giving good views, especially to the south. It is an exposed location but your car will be parked nearby for shelter.

1) 66512 climbs north with a train of concrete sleepers for Carlisle.
*March, 15:15, 80mm*

## Public Transport

Service 106/107, operate about every 2 hours and stop in Orton Village and Old Tebay. It will be about a 25-30 minute walk from either village to the location.

## Amenities

You are very close to the Tebay services on the M6 and there is unofficial access to both north and southbound sites directly from the lane.

## Accommodation

The Westmoreland Hotel is located at the northbound services. There is also a caravan park.

## Photographic Notes

There are both early morning and late evening views of northbound trains. The morning shot is from the footpath located on the east side of the bridge, the afternoon from the western side of the line, either from the lane itself or from down the driveway nearer the line.

2) 57316 coasts downhill with the loaded Chirk timber.
*Photo by Scott Borthwick, July, 15:15, 91mm*

Southbound afternoon shots can be had, wide angle from the bridge itself or with a zoom lens from the far side of the field to the north.

The nearby motorway can cause some noise, depending on the direction of the wind, which may affect the sound on videos.

# Greenholme

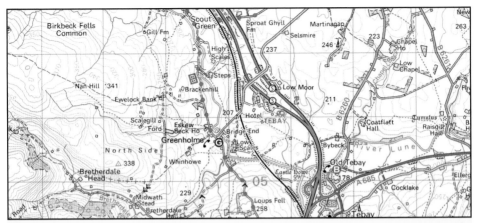

**Postcode: CA10 3TA**       **Lat N54:26:48**       **Long W02:36:53**

## Road Directions

From the M6, Junction 38: Take the B6260 towards Appleby. When you reach the village of Orton fork left onto the B6261 towards Shap.

About ½ mile after leaving the village the road turns to the right with lanes straight on and to the left. Take the left hand one which should be signposted Greenholme (though on the last visit the sign was pointing the wrong way).

After about a mile this lane will lead you under the two halves of the motorway and then to the bridge. There is plenty of room to park on the verge after the bridge.

3) Off to sample the delights of the West Highlands, 50049 and 50031 power up the climb towards Shap summit.
*March, 15:00, 80mm*

# Thrimby

## Location Notes
Also know as Little Stickland this is a quiet lane crossing a stream and the railway.

1) 221109 heads south with an Edinburgh to Birmingham working.
*February, 10:45 , 115mm*

## Public Transport
Services 106/107 operate approximately every 2 hours along the A6 from Penrith however there are no official bus stops in the area.

## Amenities
The nearest are in Shap Village with several pubs and village shops.

## Accommodation
There are several guest houses in Shap Village.

## Photographic Notes
The best shot is for afternoon trains heading south. The return wire on the overheads has recently been raised meaning it is no longer in the way of shots from the bridge. The morning shot has been spoilt

2) 390015 speeds north to Glasgow.
*February, 10:45, 70mm*

by a new signal. Although you will be looking into the light there is also a reasonable view of northbound trains. The lane is quiet so videos should not be affected by traffic noise, though the M6 is fairly close and there is not much warning of approaching trains unless the wind is in the right direction.

# Thrimby

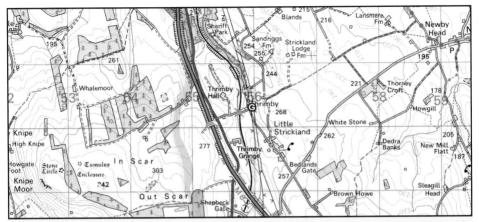

**Postcode: CA10 3DZ**     **Lat N54:34:32**     **Long W02:41:10**

## Road Directions

From the M6, Junction 39: Follow the signs for Shap (A6). When you reach the A6 turn right towards Shap
Village. Follow this road for about 5 miles passing through the village and under the motorway. Turn right
into the lane signposted Little Strickland which will lead you to the bridge.

There is limited parking after the bridge providing you take care not to block the lane or people's gateways.

3) 60047 climbs towards the summit at Shap with a Redcar to Hardendale limestone working.
*August, 19:00, 115mm*

# Great Strickland

## Location Notes
A footpath across a field near both the A6 and M6 motorways. It is quite exposed although parking on the A6 is not too far away.

1) 87026 heads north with a Glasgow express. An access road has since been built in the foreground of this shot.
   *Photo by Neil Gibson, August, 17:00, 50mm*

## Public Transport
Services 106/107 operate approximately every 2 hours along the A6 from Penrith however there are no official bus stops in the area.

## Amenities
There are none in the area. Shops can be found in Penrith about 5 miles away and there are pubs in both Hackthorpe and Great Strickland.

## Accommodation
The North Lakes Hotel is located by junction 40 of the M6, 01768 868111.

## Photographic Notes
This location offers an afternoon shot of

2) 87032 pushes a reversed Glasgow-bound express north.
   *Photo by Neil Gibson, September, 15:00, 50mm*

southbound trains with an attractive backdrop.
For videos most trains should be working hard uphill however the nearby M6 will create much background noise. There is a late summer northbound shot from the fields just behind the trees to the north of the main shot. Both locations will have the background noise from the M6.

# Great Strickland

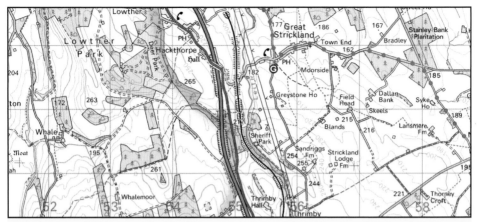

**Postcode: CA10 3DL**            **Lat N54:35:27**            **Long W02:41:50**

## Road Directions

From the south follow the directions for Thrimby through Shap Village. Continuing on the A6 after the turning for Little Strickland you pass through a wood. There is a pallet factory on the left and two footpath signs opposite each other. As you approach the brow of the hill you will see another on the right pointing over the wall which leads to the field. The road widens just after this, giving you room to park.

From Junction 40 of the M6 at Penrith take the A66 east towards Brough. At the next roundabout turn right onto the A6 towards Shap. Follow the road for about 4 miles through villages of Clifton and Hackthorpe. When you cross the motorway for the second time you pass a turning for Great Strickland on the left and then you will see the footpath sign on the left about 300 yards further on.

3) 92034 climbs towards the summit at Shap with a Carlisle to Bescot Enterprise working.
*Photo by Richard Norris, July, 19:30, 80mm*

# Cumbrian Coast

## General Notes

This line is one of the most scenic in the country as it follows the Coast of Cumbria for almost its entire length. There are several large estuaries that the line either crosses or skirts round. In some cases the railway takes a direct route across a viaduct whereas the road takes a long diversion, in others the road is more direct over a hill while the railway stays on the coast. This should be born in mind if 'chasing' a train. It is also worth noting that there is a small freight only cut-off between Dalton and Askam which misses out the loop via Barrow.

After the floods of 2009 there was a shuttle service between Workington and Maryport to provide a link for the townsfolk of Workington after the loss of their road bridges. These shuttles ceased in May 2010.

1) 156481 departs from Foxfield for Preston via Barrow.
*March, 16:30, 145mm*

## Passenger Traffic

Two operators work this line; Trans Pennine Express operates only south of Barrow using its 185 units, Northern works the whole length using a mixture of class 153 and 156 units. Between Carnforth and Barrow there is a roughly hourly service alternating between TPE and Northern, between Barrow and Millom and also between Whitehaven and Carlisle Northern provides a roughly hourly service. The section in between is nominally two hourly however there are exceptions and also extra trains as the timetable is geared to the two main sources of passengers; tourism and commuters from the BNFL site at Sellafield.

2) 37259 and 20313 head south along the coast.
*March, 13:45, 90mm*

## Freight Traffic

The main source of freight traffic is the Sellafield Nuclear Reprocessing plant. Flasks run south daily to Crewe and weekly to Heysham while northbound departures take them to plants in Scotland and Teeside. Acid tanks are another by-product which are shipped by rail, these generally depart to the north to Carlisle and there are low level waste trips between Workington Docks and Drigg. These depart Workington northwards to Maryport in order to cross over to the southbound line. Workington Docks also has an Enterprise working several times a week operated by DB Schenker.

Please note that southbound freight trains will usually use the short Barrow avoiding line so will not

3) 37427 is heading south, but has to run northbound round the sands.
*May, 12:30, 80mm*

only not pass the station but also can overtake any passenger service they may have been following.

## Occasional Traffic

The line is popular with rail tours with the Northern Belle appearing regularly in the summer and other charter trains regularly doing a circuit via both this line and the Settle to Carlisle route.

# Cumbrian Coast

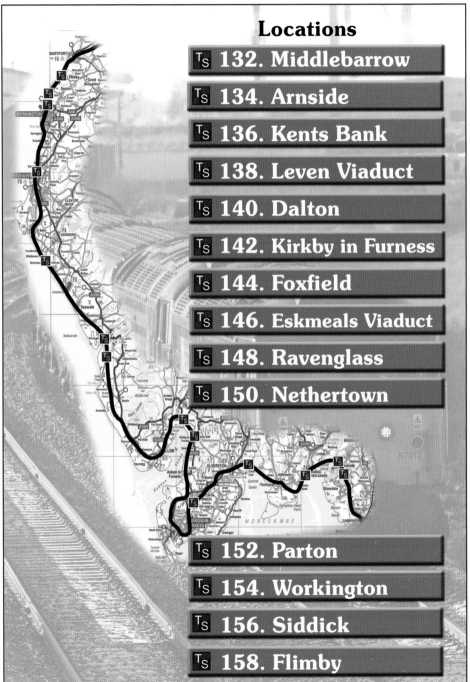

## Locations

# Middlebarrow

## Location Notes

A quiet footpath through fields alongside the railway that sees the occasional dog walker or hiker. The railway is on an embankment and separated from the field by a small stream.

1) 153313 ambles through the Cumbria countryside with a northbound Barrow-in-Furness service.
May, 17:15, 75mm

## Public Transport

Silverdale station is about a mile and a half away and is served by both Northern and Trans PennineExpress, trains from Lancaster and Carlisle.

## Amenities

There is a village shop and pub in Silverdale (though note the village is some distance from the station). Arnside is several miles away and has a much larger range of amenities including a chip shop.

2) 156471 passes the crossing to the south of the main location.
Photo by Chris Nevard, May, 18:00, 75mm

## Accommodation

The Silverdale and Arnside area is popular with tourists so there are many Bed & Breakfasts.

## Photographic Notes

This location is best in the afternoon for southbound trains (taken from the field looking up at the line) or from late afternoon through to the evening for northbound trains from the old bridge. This bridge used to lead to a crossing which is now disused and blocked off. There is a large flat field to the west so the sun has to be really low before it disappears behind the trees.

3) 156460 heads away on a northbound service. Viewed from the field.
November, 13:30, 80mm

# Middlebarrow

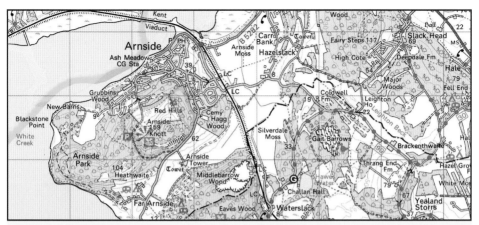

**Postcode: LA5 0JF**            **Lat N54:11:35**            **Long W02:49:08**

## Road Directions

From the M6, Junction 35: Take the A601(M) west towards Carnforth. At the end turn right onto the A6 and fork left at the next roundabout to remain on the A6 towards Milnthorpe. Pass under the main line and continue for about a mile before turning left into Nineteen Acre Lane, signposted to Silverdale and Yealand Redmayne. At the top of lane in Yealand Redmayne turn right and after Yealand Storrs turn right towards Arnside. Follow this road for several miles. When you are in the woods you will come to a junction signed right to Arnside, ignore this and continue straight on. You will come to a junction, in Waterslack, where a dead-end road on the right will turn you back to Middlebarrow. Turn down here and continue to the end. There is room for two cars to park by the crossing or at the left hand corner just before.

Continue on foot over the crossing into Middlebarrow Quarry and turn right through the woods by the railway. Fork right in the woods and over a bridge over the stream. The footpath then runs alongside the railway through the field.

4) Taken from a small wooden bridge across the stream, 156464 heads south with a local working to Lancaster.
*Photo by Chris Nevard, May, 17:00, 40mm*

# Kent Viaduct, Arnside

## Location Notes
Arnside is a pleasant village located on the edge of a wide tidal estuary at the top of Morecambe Bay which the line crosses by a long viaduct.

1) 185122 heads east across the Kent Viaduct with a southbound Manchester Airport working.
*April, 14:15, 45mm*

There is also a high hill above the town which affords good views towards the Lakeland Fells. It is a good place to keep the family entertained while you wait for trains as there is a long promenade with a range of shops.

## Public Transport
Arnside station is served roughly hourly by trains from Manchester and Lancaster to Barrow.

## Amenities
There is a wide range of small shops, pubs and a good fish and chip shop along the promenade.

## Accommodation
There are several hotels and a range of Bed & Breakfasts in the village.

2) 153358 and156483 head north to Carlisle.
*March, 10:45, 50mm*

## Photographic Notes
The light is best for southbound trains, which will be travelling east at this point, from mid-morning to mid-afternoon, however when the sun is off the front there is a range of wide angle views of the viaduct possible. There are shots from the foreshore, the promenade, or, for the more adventurous, by climbing Arnside Knott which is the big hill behind the town.

The promenade can be very busy on nice days which is worth bearing in mind if videoing.

Trains rumble loudly as they cross the viaduct.

3)156468 comes off the eastern end of the viaduct.
*February, 13:45, 135mm*

# Kent Viaduct, Arnside

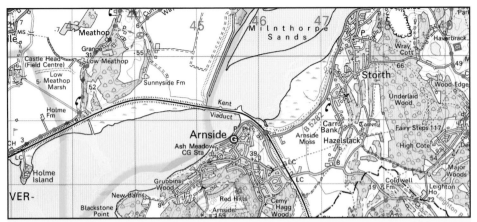

**Postcode: LA5 0HD**    **Lat N54:12:17**    **Long W02:50:01**

## Road Directions

From the M6, Junction 35: Take the A601(M) west for a mile to its end before turning right onto the A6 for Milnthorpe. Fork left at next roundabout and pass under the main line. Continue for around 5 miles until you reach Milnthorpe and turn left at the traffic light in the village onto the B5282 to Arnside. Pass through Sandside and just before the end of the road you pass under the Barrow line. Turn right after the bridge and you will see Arnside Station. Follow along the wall of the railway and you will reach the promenade. There is plenty of free parking on the promenade or there is parking on the foreshore just as the road bends left onto the front.

4) 156441 heads for Lancaster. Viewed from the south-eastern corner of the viaduct.
*March, 10:45, 40mm*

# Kents Bank

## Location Notes

A quiet crossing giving vehicle access to the foreshore in a quiet residential area. The line approaches from the north along the sea wall. The tide no longer comes up to the land following movements of the channel, however the grassy beach can still be very muddy.

1) 156480 conveys convivial Cumbrian commuters to Preston in the am.
*March, 06:45, 80mm*

## Public Transport

Kents Bank is the nearest station, about ½ mile away, though not all trains stop there. Grange-over-Sands station is about a mile away which all Barrow trains serve.

## Amenities

There are none at the location however Grange is 5 minutes away by car and has a range of shops and pubs and take-aways.

## Accommodation

Being on the edge of the south lakes there is plenty of tourist accommodation in and around Grange.

2) 37510, 37194, 37038 and 47237 head flasks towards Sellafield.
*November, 10:00, 65mm*

## Photographic Notes

As the line curves round here to almost be heading south it is one of the few locations where northbound (to Barrow) trains can be photographed with the sun on the front from early morning until late afternoon. The sun will be head on around 13:00.

There are shots from both sides of the crossing looking to the north. There is a southbound shot of the train passing the crossing if you walk along the shore and climb the sea wall.

# Kents Bank

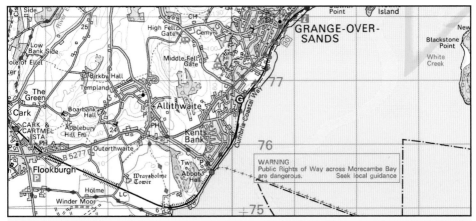

**Postcode: LA11 7AF**     **Lat N54:10:51**     **Long W02:55:08**

## Road Directions

From the M6, Junction 36: Take the A590 towards Kendal for 3 miles and at the next junction turn left onto the A590 towards Barrow. It is about 6 miles to the next roundabout where you should turn left onto the B5277 heading for Grange. The road turns left at the mini-roundabout in Lindale Village. Head into Grange-over-Sands, passing the station on your left. Turn left at the mini-roundabout and drive through Main Street. At the end of Main Street bear left at the mini roundabout towards Flookburgh. Continue along this road, following it you will pass the Cumbrian Fire and Rescue station on your left. Then you will see a large red building, Cartmel Grange, on the right on top of the hill. When you see this turn left down the road signposted to the Promenade. This is Cart Lane. Follow it down and to the right. The level crossing is on the left opposite Carter Road.

3) *Tornado* heads around the coast with a tour to Carlisle, before returning to Crewe via the S&C.
   *Photo by Marcus Dawson, April, 10:15, 120mm*

# Leven Viaduct, Plumpton

## Location Notes

On the edge of the Leven Estuary this is a road that leads down to the beach. It is in a quiet area with farmland to the west and the estuary to the east. Plumpton used to be the junction of the line to Lakeside and a signal post still exists even though the line has been closed since 1965.

1) 175004 and 007 make their way west across the 490 metres and 49 arches of the Leven viaduct.
*March, 14:45, 120mm*

## Public Transport

Ulverston station is served by workings from Carnforth and is a 30 to 45 minute walk away.

## Amenities

There are none at the location. Ulverston is about 3 miles away and has a wide range of shops and supermarkets.

## Photographic Notes

There are two locations here. Shots from the foreshore looking towards the viaduct have the best light in the afternoon for trains heading towards Barrow. The viaduct was refurbished in 2006 and is now cleaner, but with a blue railing that differs slightly from the image shown. From the same location there is a sweeping view of Carnforth bound trains.

The road crosses the railway on a bridge which gives good views looking towards Ulverston with the lighthouse on the hill. The light is best here in the morning for trains heading towards Carnforth. The eastbound view from the bridge is more limited due to trees and the curve of the line.

2) 60069 heads east with a coal train to Padiham power station.
*Photo by Neil Harvey, June, 11:00, 80mm*

3) 156443 heads east past the former Plumpton Junction.
*June, 11:00, 80mm*

# Leven Viaduct, Plumpton

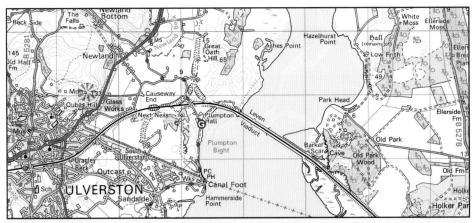

**Postcode: LA12 7QN**                **Lat N54:11:58**                **Long W03:02:42**

## Road Directions

From M6, Junction 36: Take the A590 towards Kendal turning left after about 3 miles at the next junction in order to remain on the A590 towards Barrow.

Keep on the A590 for approximately 17 miles. You will reach Greenodd with the A5092 to Workington on the right. Continue straight on and after the second short stretch of dual-carriageway take the next left onto the lane towards Plumpton. Turn left again at the end of this lane and after ½ mile you will come to two bridges, the first the track bed of the line to Lakeside, the second the current line. There is room to park on the bridge. Continuing past here the road becomes unmade and leads to the foreshore.

4) 60066 crosses the River Leven with Padiham to Workington coal empties - long since ceased.
Photo by Neil Harvey, June, 15:00, 95mm

# Dalton

## Location Notes

There are two locations here. #1 is a road bridge by the railway station, #2, is a road bridge at the other end of Dalton Tunnel and near the junction of the freight only Barrow avoiding line.

1) At bridge #1, 156451 slows for Dalton-in-Furness station with a service to Carlisle.
*April, 13:30, 80mm*

## Public Transport

Dalton station, opposite #1, is about a 15-20 minute walk to bridge #2.

## Amenities

Dalton has a wide range of pubs and shops.

## Accommodation

The Chequers Hotel is located near bridge #2.

## Photographic Notes

Bridge #1 gives a good afternoon view of trains heading towards Barrow. The bridge is on a road junction and there is no pavement on that side, so it would be unsuitable for video tripods.

Bridge #2 gives good views in both directions. In early morning the light will be on the front for trains leaving the junction heading towards Dalton. Here the line is tree-lined so shadows will be a problem.

2) #2, 185133 with a westbound train from Barrow.
*April, 12:45, 80mm*

From mid-morning onwards the light is better for trains coming out of the tunnel though this angle is quite tight. There is also little warning of approaching trains. The best shot will be on a summer evening, taking the train emerging from the tunnel.

The road crosses the line on a large bridge. There is a crash barrier on the western side separating the pavement from the road so it is not easy to cross from side to side.

The road is fairly busy so traffic noise will feature on videos.

# Dalton

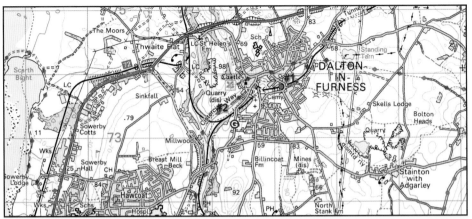

**Postcode: LA13 0PE**          **Lat N54:09:03**          **Long W03:11:23**

## Road Directions

From the M6, Junction 36: Follow the A590 Kendal for 3 miles turning left to remain on the A590 towards Barrow. Continue on this road until you reach Ulverston, about 20 miles. After passing through the town you pass through Swarthmoor and cross the railway for the second time. Turn left at the roundabout signposted to Dalton. Pass along the main street and turn left by the White Horse onto the road signposted to the Chequers Hotel. The bridge is just after the hotel and car showroom, the road is wide enough for you to be able to park easily before the bridge #2. The road to Dalton station and Bridge #1 is signposted off the main street.

3) #2, Having just come off the Barrow avoiding line, behind the signal box, 66423 and 427 head towards Carnforth.
*April, 13:00, 200mm*

# Kirkby in Furness

## Location Notes

A quiet rural village on the edge of the Duddon Estuary. It can be quite exposed in winter and there is no shelter on the edge of the estuary.

1) A stitched panorama shows off the Lake District as 67001 heads south with the Northern Belle to Manchester.
*June, 18:30, 50mm (original inset)*

## Public Transport

Kirkby-in-Furness is served, as a request stop, by most trains between Barrow-in-Furness, Millom and Carlisle.

## Amenities

The Ship Inn is next to the station. It is closed on Mondays, Tuesdays and Wednesdays. The Burlington Inn is on the main road and there is a local shop opposite this.

## Accommodation

The Ship Inn has a 16 bed hostel.

## Photographic Notes

Photos can be taken from two locations and the light is normally best for Barrow-bound trains. Near the station you can either stand near the old goods dock at the station, light best in the morning, or from the foreshore as the train rounds the curve. The light for this will be best from late morning until late afternoon. About 500 yards to the south there is a foot crossing and from here, or from further down the shoreline, shots can be taken from mid afternoon until the evening. As the estuary is to the east here there will be no shadows until the sun sets. The location will be suitable for videoing as there is little background noise.

2) 156428 heads south with a Preston service.
*June, 18:00, 65mm*

3) 20312 and 20316 take a single flask to Crewe.
*Photo by Scott Borthwick, September, 09:30, 50mm*

# Kirkby in Furness

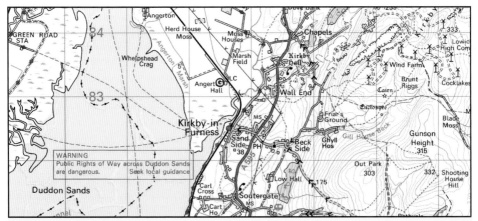

**Postcode: LA17 7XA**          **Lat N54:14:14**          **Long W03:11:10**

## Road Directions

From the M6, Junction 36: Follow the A590 Kendal for 3 miles turning left at the next junction to remain on the A590 towards Barrow. Continue for about 17 miles until you reach Greenodd where you should turn right onto the A5092 signposted Workington. Follow this road for 6 miles until Grizebeck. At the bottom of a steep hill turn left onto the A595 towards Barrow. It is about 1½ miles to the start of Kirkby-in-Furness and a further ½ mile to the village. Turn right by the Burlington Inn and the station is at the bottom of the lane. For the station locations park here. The road to the right will lead you to the old goods dock; the station footbridge and crossing gives access to the foreshore.

The other location is reached by the road on the left, the farm/foot crossing is on the right opposite the Sandside Gospel Hall.

4) 156438 heads south towards Kirkby-in-Furness station with a local working from Carlisle.
*March, 08:45, 45mm*

# Foxfield

## Location Notes

Foxfield is little more than a few houses, a pub and a railway station, though it acts as the railhead for the town of Broughton. The station is located by the main road at the head of the Duddon Estuary.

1) 66417 and 66426 head south with empties from Sellafield bound for Crewe.
*March, 17:00, 170mm*

## Public Transport

The station, a request stop, is served by trains between Barrow, Millom and Carlisle.
There is an infrequent bus service linking the station with Broughton, which is 2 miles away.

## Amenities

The Prince of Wales pub opposite the station serves sandwiches and pasties. Broughton has a range of small shops and pubs.

## Accommodation

There is a selection of hotels and guest houses in Broughton. The Prince of Wales also does B&B.

2) 153328 ambles south, away from Foxfield Station.
*September, 12:15, 135mm*

## Photographic Notes

There are two locations here. One is by the level crossing just east of the station, the other is ¼ mile further down the road that crosses this crossing.
Note that the crossing has a gate keeper who only opens the gate when needed by a car. There is a bell to attract their attention.
The sun will be head-on mid morning and after this it will favour trains heading towards Barrow for most of the day. By evening the sun will have moved round onto the front of trains from the other direction.
Down the lane the railway runs at a higher level than the lane, separated by a stone wall. It is possible to climb this wall without too much effort or shots can be taken side-on from the foreshore.
Traffic on the main road will feature on sound recordings taken by the crossing but the lane is very quiet.

# Foxfield

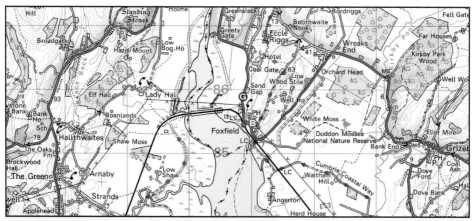

**Postcode: LA20 6BX**        **Lat N54:15:39**        **Long W03:13:12**

## Road Directions

From the M6, junction 36: Follow the A590 towards Kendal turning off at the first junction to remain on the A590 towards Barrow. After 17 miles turn right at Greenodd onto the A5092 which is joined by the A595 at Grizebeck. Continue on the A595 and as you enter Foxfield you will see a sign for a gated crossing on the left.

There is room to park by the crossing. Go over the crossing and follow the lane alongside the railway to the south to reach the second location.

3) 20313 and 20314 head east with a south-bound working to Heysham.
*September, 16:15, 45mm*

# Eskmeals Viaduct

## Location Notes

This location is a viaduct crossing a tidal estuary just south of Ravenglass.

1) 37417 and 37401 cruise across the estuary at low tide with the 'Lake District Explorer' from Ravenglass to Cardiff.
*Photo by Steve Philpott, June, 14:15, 35mm*

## Public Transport

Bootle station is 3 miles away to the south.

## Amenities

There are none in the immediate area. There is a pub and a butchers shop, a mile away on the main road. There are also pubs and tea rooms in Ravenglass which is about 3 miles away by road.

## Accommodation

There are several hotels in Ravenglass.

## Photographic Notes

There are angles here from the foreshore and from next to the line. The light is best in the afternoon for trains heading south towards Barrow-in-Furness.

The old station is next to the viaduct and by climbing up the bank to the old wall of the platform you can get shots of trains crossing the viaduct.

The area is very quiet so is good for videoing though there is the possibility of gunfire from the nearby firing range.

2) 20312 and 20306 with a Sellafield to Crewe move.
*Photo by Scott Borthwick, September, 15:45, 50mm*

3) River becomes road. 153352 and 331 pass by.
*March, 11:15, 40mm*

# Eskmeals Viaduct

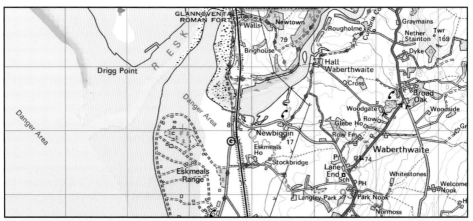

**Postcode: LA19 5YG**        **Lat N54:20:08**        **Long W02:34:18**

## Road Directions

The main Barrow to Workington Road, the A595, passes a mile away. From the south you pass through
Bootle. After 3 miles you reach Wabberthwaite. Turn left after the Brown Cow Inn towards Newbiggin.
Follow this lane and it passes under the viaduct. There is plenty of room to park after the bridge.
The road can be flooded during high tides, see picture 3, which makes it impassable. When this happens
you will need to come via Bootle station and the coastal road past the Eskmeals Firing Range.

4) 20308, 20314, 37611 and three nuclear flasks cross Eskmeals Viaduct with a Sellafield-Crewe working.
*Photo by Scott Borthwick, September, 16:30, 55mm*

# Ravenglass

## Location Notes

Ravenglass is a small town on the River Esk. It is geared towards tourism as it is the start of the Ravenglass and Eskdale minuture steam railway.

1) 156451 heads north to Carlisle with a local working from Barrow-in-Furness.
   *April, 15:45, 70mm*

## Public Transport

Ravenglass station is served by trains from both Carlisle and Barrow.

## Amenities

There is a good pub located in the station, The Ratty Arms, which does pub lunches. There is also a Tea Room in the village and a cafe on the Ravenglass and Eskdale Railway station. Free public toilets are provided at the car park.

## Accommodation

There is a hotel and several guest houses in Ravenglass village.

2) 156480 heads south over the estuary.
   *April, 14:00, 135mm*

## Photographic Notes

The best views are of trains crossing the bridge over the River Esk. The sun is right for southbound trains heading towards Barrow from about 12:00 onwards. Evenings will favour northbound workings from the other bank of the river. The line crosses on a short viaduct and shots can be taken from the promenade. A footpath crosses the bridge enabling you to reach the other bank. There is a thin telegraph wire along the western side but it is not too intrusive. In the morning there is a shot looking down to the viaduct and estuary from the field near the top of the road, by the electricity pylon.

3) 156481 heads north to Carlisle.
   *March, 12:15, 210mm*

# Ravenglass

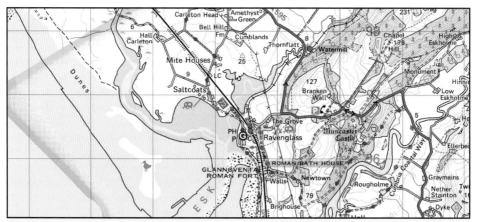

**Postcode: CA18 1SW**          **Lat N54:21:27**          **Long W03:24:41**

## Road Directions

Ravenglass is located just off the main A595 Barrow to Workington road. From the south the turning is on the left just after you pass Muncaster Castle. It is well signposted. After you pass under the Ravenglass and Eskdale Railway and main lines, head along the promenade and follow signs for the large free car park (there is an alternative Pay and Display one at the Ravenglass and Eskdale Railway station).

4) 37609, 37610, 20313 and 37607 head nuclear flasks forming a Sellafield to Crewe working over Ravenglass Viaduct.
*Photo by Scott Borthwick, May, 15:45, 105mm*

# Nethertown

## Location Notes
Nethertown is a small hamlet of cottages and static caravans on cliffs in a sparsly populated part of the coast between Whitehaven and Sellafield.

1) Catching the Irish Sea breeze, 37682 leads 37510 towards Sellafield with the southbound 'Cumbrian Coaster'.
*Photo by Neil Gibson, September, 15:30, 45mm*

## Public Transport
Nethertown station is a request stop served by 4 trains a day running between Barrow and Carlisle.

## Amenities
There are none in the immediate area. Egremont is about 4 miles away and has a good selection of shops and public houses.

## Photographic Notes
There are two locations here. The first is near the station on a public footpath that climbs from the station up the cliff. This gives a good morning view of southbound trains passing through the station. There is also a view the other way looking towards the second location. This viewpoint consists of a bridge leading to a small headland with a few small houses. Here you can photograph northbound trains from the bridge (the sun will only come round fully in the evening) or southbound trains from the northern end of the houses looking towards the station. As the railway is alongside the sea the sun will remain out until it reaches the horizon. It is a very quiet area so good for videoing.

2) 156443 with a Barrow-in-Furness to Carlisle local.
*March, 15:00, 40mm*

3) 156438 heads north along the coast to Carlisle,
*June, 15:00, 50mm*

# Nethertown

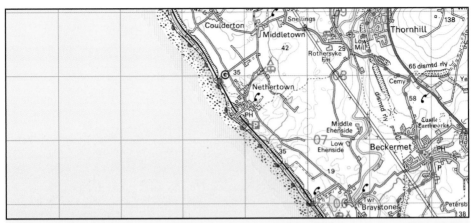

**Postcode: CA22 2UQ**       **Lat N54:27:18**       **Long W03:33:51**

## Road Directions

Heading north up the A595 from Barrow turn left onto the B5345 about ½ mile after you pass the roundabout leading to the southern gate of Sellafield. Go over a small stone bridge and follow the road to the right, signposted Nethertown station. After about ¾ mile turn left towards Middletown. Go through the village following the signs for Nethertown. For the first location turn right at the lane signposted to the station. Go straight on at the next junction and the track drops steeply down the cliff, round a hairpin bend, to the station. There is room for about 2 cars at the station. The footpath goes off the south end of the platform. To reach the second location go past the turning to the station and turn left in the village. Take the next right, at the triangular junction and this lane leads over the bridge. There is room to park just after the bridge and more parking and room to turn at the bottom of the cliff.

4) Peak hour on the coast as 20310 and 20312 warble their way south towards journey's end at Sellafield.
*June, 08:30, 80mm*

# Parton

## Location Notes
A small suburb just to the north of the town of Whitehaven with views from the hills or the line side.

1) 37682 and 37510 return south with the 'Cumbrian Coaster'. Viewed from the sea side of the line.
*Photo by Carl Grocott, September, 15:45, 55mm*

## Public Transport
Parton is served by trains from Barrow and Carlisle.

## Amenities
The Lowther Arms is just across the green from the station. There is a range of supermarkets and fast food outlets in Whitehaven just to the south.

## Photographic Notes
The primary shots here are from the roads to the south of the village. Here you are afforded sweeping views of the line to both the north and south but the light will only really suit southbound workings until early afternoon. There is a large gravelled open space between the position and the line so it is better suited to telephoto shots than wide angle views.

A second location to the north of the station offers a shot of southbound workings in the afternoon.

To reach this location use the station underpass to gain access to the west side of the line and follow the footpath north up the coast. There are options along the path but there is a set of semaphores, just before the industrial unit, close to the curve.

2) 20312 & 313 skirt the coast line south to Sellafield.
*Photo by Peter Foster, July, 10:45, 300mm*

3) Dwarfed by the coastal hills 156469 heads south.
*Photo by Marcus Dawson, April, 13:00, 200mm*

# Parton

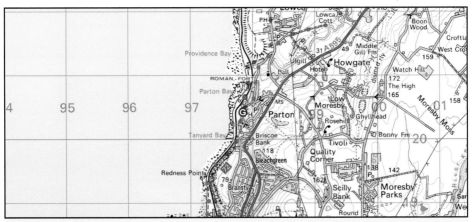

**Postcode: CA28 6NY**          **Lat N54:34:11**          **Long W03:34:57**

## Road Directions

From the north take the A595 south past Workington. The road changes from a dual carriageway to single carriageway at a roundabout after Distington. Shortlly after this, turn right and take the road into Parton and continue along the road until it starts to climb back up. There is a bus stop opposite a right turn that leads back down to the village.

From the south take the A595 out of Whitehaven. Shortly after a parking/viewing area on the left and a sharp corner you will see a bus stop on the left and then the left turn down to the village.

This road has the vantage points, but it is best to drive to the bottom, park and walk back up.

4) An Irish Sea back-drop for the acid tanks, 37029 and 37229, as they head for Sellafield.
*June, 10:00, 80mm*

# Derwent Junction, Workington

## Location Notes

This location is a bridge that carries a road to the docks. It can be busy with lorries and cars.
It will be a fairly exposed place in winter with not much shelter except for your car which can be parked next to the bridge.

1) 66420 top & tails out of Workington Docks with 66426 on a low-level nuclear waste movement to Drigg.
*December, 11:15, 70mm*

## Public Transport

It is about a 20 minute walk from Workington station which is on the southern side of the river.

## Amenities

The Dunmail shopping centre is on the A596 just north of the location with a variety of shops and cafes. There is also a Tesco store on the southen side of the river.

## Accommodation

The Morven House B&B is located about a mile north on the main road.

## Photographic Notes

The best shot is for southbound trains and pictures can be taken at most times of day, although the sun will be head on around dinner time.

2) 37610 and 47501 head a shuttle south.
*December, 14:15, 250mm*

Shots of northbound trains can also be taken into the sun. Early in the evening the sun should move round far enough to get sun on the nose for these.

The bridge spans Derwent Junction where the line from the docks joins and shots can be had of trains departing, though this would be best in dull weather.

Passing road traffic will be a problem for videographers.

# Derwent Junction, Workington

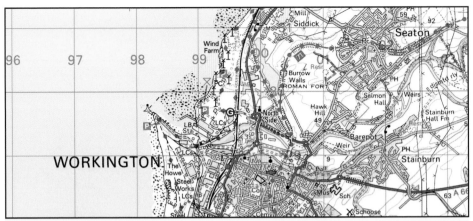

**Postcode: CA14 1JJ**        **Lat N54:39:08**        **Long W03:33:26**

## Road Directions

From the M6 at Penrith: Take the A66 towards Cockermouth, skirting the town on the A595 before turning left onto the A594 to Maryport.

On reaching Maryport take the A596 towards Workington. After 2 miles you will pass Flimby station on the right then a further mile brings the Dunmail Shopping Centre on the left. You will come to a large roundabout shortly afterwards. Turn right at this and this road will lead you across the bridge.

Parking is possible for several cars on the right immediately after the bridge.

3) 37259 and 47790, with 57004 on the tail of a southbound shuttle. The former temporary station is in the background.
*December, 11:15, 225mm*

# Siddick

## Location Notes

A very exposed footpath, with no immediate shelter, on banking between a wind farm, the railway and the sea. Used mainly by dog walkers, the farmer or maintenance workers in the area.

1) 37510 top & tails with 47501 on a temporary flood shuttle service between Maryport and Workington.
*December, 11:00, 80mm*

## Public Transport

Flimby station is approximately 1 mile north of the location along the A596.
Stagecoach, services 30/31 and 300, operate along the main road from Workignton and Maryport.

## Amenities

There is the Dunmail shopping centre on the A596 ½ mile south of the location with a variety of shops and cafes.

## Accommodation

The Morven House Bed & Breakfast is located nearby on the main road.

2) 66426 and 66420 with a Workington Docks trip.
*December, 11:45, 100mm*

## Photographic Notes

Photographs can be taken in both directions at most times of day. The best shot is generally of southbound trains taken from the north end of the embankment mid morning to just after lunch. In late afternoon it is possible to take southbound shots from the footpath alongside the line on the seaward side. Northbound shots are also possible but except for very early morning will be into the light.
Wind noise should be the only problem for videographers.

3) 57004, 47790 and 37259 with a northbound shuttle.
*December, 11:45, 90mm*

# Siddick

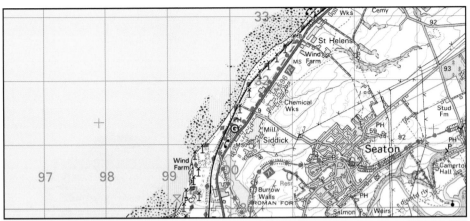

**Postcode: CA14 1LA**          **Lat N54:40:11**          **Long W03:32:60**

## Road Directions

From the M6 at Penrith take the A66 towards Cockermouth, skirting the town on the A595 before turning left onto the A594 to Maryport. On reaching Maryport take the A596 towards Workington. You will, after a few miles, pass Flimby station on the right then 5 windmills on the right followed by a sewage works. Just after this is a turning on the left signposted Seaton. Immediately opposite this turning is a track on the right leading down towards the railway.

There is room for several cars to park at the end. A stile leads you onto the embankment.

4) The more usual motive power on the Cumbrian coast route. 156444 breezes past the Siddick wind farm.
*December, 12:45, 45mm*

# Flimby

## Location Notes
Flimby is a small ribbon settlement located on the coastal strip north of Workington spread out alongside the road and railway. The village is very quiet with just one pub and a village shop.

1) 57012 powers north with the temporary shuttle service for Maryport.
*April, 10:45, 325mm*

## Public Transport
Stagecoach, services 30/31 and 300, operate along the main road from Maryport and Workington. Flimby station, a request stop, is served roughly hourly by services from Carlisle.

## Amenities
There is the Dunmail shopping centre on the A596 2 miles south nearer Workington, Maryport is a similar distance north.
There is a village shop opposite the station serving pies, drinks and snacks.

2) 37610 thrashes south on a shuttle to Workington.
*December, 12:00, 80mm*

## Accommodation
The Morven House Bed & Breakfast is about a mile south the main road.

## Photographic Notes
About 50 yards north of the station there is a small under bridge. By carefully climbing onto the retaining wall shots can be had in both directions, southbound will be best in the morning, northbound generally into the light. A later afternoon shot can be had from the foreshore to the south of the station leaning over the fence, also a morning shot can be had at the southern end of the village on the main road. Whilst not essential, a step ladder will be an advantage here to get more of the sea in the background.
Traffic noise, from the A596, will affect video sound tracks.

# Flimby

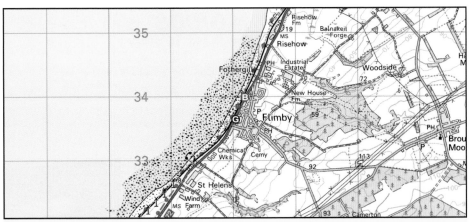

**Postcode: CA15 8QW**          **Lat N54:41:20**          **Long W03:31:17**

## Road Directions

From the M6 at Penrith take the A66 towards Cockermouth, skirting the town on the A595 before turning left onto the A594 to Maryport. On reaching Maryport take the A596 towards Workington. You will, after about two miles, see Flimby station on the right. There are plenty of side streets available to park on.

If you require the shot at the southern end of the village, as you approach the '40' signs marking the end of Flimby, you can see a grassy area on the right. It is possible to park on here, although take care not to get your car in the way of your own shot!

3) 47501 powers away from the stop at Flimby station with a southbound shuttle to Workington.
*January, 15:15, 160mm*

# Further Reading...

## GRIDS
### The Class 56 Story

Features their conception in the early 1970s to the preservation scene of today. The Grids have captured the imagination and devotion of enthusiasts nationwide. This is the complete story of their varied and unusual lives.

**128 pages
200 photos, diagrams and tables
A4 softback
Over 60,000 words**

## BRITS ABROAD

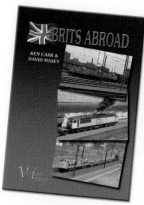

This is the only book to take an in-depth look at the diesel and electric locos that have worked on our national network and, at some point in their lives, overseas as well. From the LMS shunters involved in the Second World War to the Bulgaria-bound 87s, and everything in between, this is a fascinating subject which was long overdue for serious review.

**100 pages
200 photos, diagrams and tables
A4 softback
Over 35,000 words**

## We also produce a wide range of DVDs

### Full details can be found on our website...

# www.visionsinternational.biz

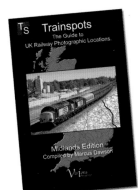
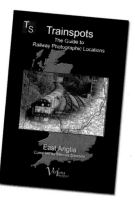

# Index

The locations in this book are listed in alphabetical order with relevant page numbers. The coloured squares refer to the coloured chapter tabs.